Conducting the Java Job Interview
IT Manager Guide for Java with Interview Questions

Jeffrey M. Hunter

I dedicate this book to my wife Melody and my son Alex whose love and support made this book possible.

--- Jeff Hunter

Conducting the Java Job Interview
IT Manager Guide for Java with Interview Questions

By Jeffrey M. Hunter

Copyright © 2004 by Rampant TechPress. All rights reserved.

Printed in the United States of America.

Published by: Rampant TechPress, Kittrell, North Carolina, USA

IT Job Interview Series: Book #1

Series Editor: Don Burleson

Editors: John Lavender, Janet Burleson and Sheila Jenkins

Production Editor: Teri Wade

Cover Design: Janet Burleson

Illustrations: Mike Reed

Printing History: April 2004 First Printing, January 2007 Second Printing

Java, J2EE, J2SE, J2ME, and all Java-based marks are trademarks or registered trademarks of Sun Microsystems Corporation. *IT Job Interview* is a registered Trademark of Rampant TechPress.

Flame Warriors illustrations are copyright © by Mike Reed Illustrations Inc.

Many of the designations used by computer vendors to distinguish their products are claimed as Trademarks. All names known to Rampant TechPress to be trademark names appear in this text as initial caps.

The information provided by the authors of this work is believed to be accurate and reliable, but because of the possibility of human error by our authors and staff, Rampant TechPress cannot guarantee the accuracy or completeness of any information included in this work and is not responsible for any errors, omissions, or inaccurate results obtained from the use of information or scripts in this work.

ISBN: 0-9744355-8-9

ISBN-13: 978-0-9744355-8-9

Library of Congress Control Number: 2004101888

Table of Contents

Using the Online Code Depot

Your purchase of this book provides you with complete access to the online code depot that contains the sample questions and answers.

All of the job questions in this book are located at the following URL:

www.rampant.cc/job_java.htm

All of the sample tests and questions in this book will be available for download, ready to use for your next interview.

If you need technical assistance in downloading or accessing the scripts, please contact Rampant TechPress at info@rampant.cc

Conventions Used in this Book

It is critical for any technical publication to follow rigorous standards and employ consistent punctuation conventions to make the text easy to read.

However, this is not an easy task. Within Java there are many types of notations that can confuse a reader. Some Java technologies, such as J2SE and J2SE SDK, are always spelled in CAPITAL letters, while Java parameters and procedures have varying naming conventions in the Java documentation. It is also important to remember that many Java commands are case sensitive, and are always left in their original executable form, and never altered with italics or capitalization. Hence, all Rampant TechPress books follow these conventions:

Source Code – Anything that might appear in a Java program, including code snippets, keywords, method names, variables names, class names, and interface names will use a `monospaced font`.

New Terms – An *Italics font* will be used for all new terms, book titles and for emphasis.

Parameters and Placeholders – A *lowercase italics* font will be used to identify any command-line parameters or placeholders required by the user.

Commands and Java Programs – A `**bold monospaced font**` will be used to identify Java binaries or command-line applications that will need to be typed by the user.

Products – All products that are known to the author are capitalized according to the vendor specifications (IBM, DBXray, Sun Microsystems, etc). All names known by Rampant TechPress to be trademark names appear in this text as initial caps. References to UNIX are always made in uppercase.

Acknowledgements

This type of highly technical reference book requires the dedicated efforts of many people. Even though I am the author, my work ends when I deliver the content. After each chapter is delivered, several Java programmers carefully review and correct the technical content.

After the technical review, experienced copy editors polish the grammar and syntax. The finished work is then reviewed as page proofs and turned over to the production manager, who arranges the creation of the online code depot and manages the cover art, printing distribution, and warehousing.

In short, the author played a small role in the development of this book, and I need to thank and acknowledge everyone who helped bring this book to fruition:

- **John Lavender**, for the production management, including the coordination of the cover art, page proofing, printing, and distribution.

- **Teri Wade**, for her help in the production of the page proofs.

- **Janet Burleson**, for her exceptional cover design and graphics.

- **Jennifer Adkins**, for her assistance with the web site, and the online shopping cart for this book.

- **Sheila Jenkins**, for her expert page-proofing services.

With my sincerest thanks,

Jeffrey M. Hunter

Preface

After interviewing countless candidates for Java-related positions, I am aware that it is getting harder to locate and retain qualified Java professionals. You must cull the best fit from hundreds of résumés. Success depends upon knowing exactly which skills you need, and verifying that each candidate possesses acceptable levels of those skills.

That's where this book can help you. For both the new IT manager and the seasoned VP, the levels within the Java programming position will be explained to illustrate screening and interview techniques. Some common misconceptions about the Java programming position will be clarified and tips will be provided on how to interview a candidate for this type of position.

Large numbers of Java neophytes are obtaining Java programming certification through the Sun Certified Java Programmer (SCJP) and Sun Certified Java Developer (SCJD) program. This overabundance of Sun Certified Java programmers makes it more important than ever to evaluate every candidate's experience and working knowledge of the Java language.

Few IT managers, especially in smaller companies, have extensive formal training in interviewing and hiring techniques. Most interviewers' primary full-time responsibilities lie elsewhere. It is a fact that most IT managers do not even have a clear idea of the skills and personal characteristics their candidate should possess, much less an effective process for screening potential employees. Yet nothing is more crucial to the success of the organization than doing everything possible to ensure that the selected candidate is the best fit for the available position.

This book will provide effective techniques for finding committed employees who are able to function at a high level on the job. By eliminating guesswork and rejecting the random hit-or-miss approach that is based on the instincts of the interviewer and little else, the employer can hire confidently.

To help find, hire, and retain suitable Java professionals, background evaluation tips will be provided for identifying the best candidates. For the technical interview, sample questions and answers are also provided. A non-technical evaluation section is provided to help determine whether the candidate's personality is a good match for the organization and whether the candidate will be able to integrate scamlessly with your shop's particular culture.

Of course, there is no magic formula for determining if a candidate can perform properly, and no single screening test to ensure that you will properly evaluate a candidate's ability. However, if the employer and candidate are properly prepared, then filling the position successfully becomes less of a risk.

It is my hope that this book will become an indispensable tool for identifying, interviewing, and hiring top-notch Java professionals.

IMPORTANT NOTE:

The intention of this section is not to provide a comprehensive technical exam, and the technical questions in this code depot are only intended to be examples. The only way to accurately evaluate the technical skills of a job applicant is to employ the services of an experienced person and conduct an in-depth technical interview and skills assessment.

Also note that the expected answers from the questions are highly dependent upon the version of the product and the candidates' interpretation of the question. We have tried to make the questions as version neutral as possible, but each new release of every product brings hundreds of changes and new features, and these example questions may not be appropriate for your version. An experienced technical person should always administer the interview questions presented in this book.

Java Programmer Evaluation

Introduction

Since its official debut by Sun Microsystems in 1995, Java has matured from a tool that makes Applets to an enterprise development environment able to support today's most mission-critical applications. With its promise of platform independence, reliable security, and robust support for distributed network environments, companies of all types are embracing and adopting the Java platform for developing their next-generation IT applications. A survey performed in the year 2000 revealed more than 40% of Fortune 500 companies use Java. In 2003, this number has risen to well over 85%, and continues to grow.

One of the results of Java's popularity is an ever-increasing demand for top-notch Java programmers and developers. However, culling experienced Java talent is difficult given Java's brief existence in the marketplace. As more companies continue to utilize Java for their businesses, the demand for skilled Java programmers increases. However, this mushrooming need for Java programmers has created a vastly disparate job pool. Job skills range from software engineers with PhDs in Information Systems from top U.S. universities and 20 years' experience, to semi-literate Java programming trainees with 90 days' experience.

The result of the explosive growth of the Java industry is a two-tiered job market. Many top-rated universities teach Java as part of their undergraduate CS or IT curriculum and produce Java programmers for career tracks in large corporations. At the same time, trade schools and community colleges educate hundreds of thousands of Java programmers and developers. No matter what the economic climate, large corporations actively recruit their entry-level talent for their mission-critical systems development from prestigious universities.

Written with the IT manager in mind, this book provides a useful insight into the techniques as to what characteristics make a successful Java professional job candidate.

Preparing the Java Programming Job Offering

One of the points that I repeatedly make is that top-notch Java programmers are hard to find and well compensated, while mediocre Java programmers are easy to find and hire.

On the high end, Java programmers with over 10 years' IT programming experience and graduate degrees typically command salaries ranging from $78,000 to $101,000 per year, depending on geographical location. For Principle Software Engineering consultants with strong Java experience and broad exposure in mission-critical areas, the sky is the limit. Certification also plays a critical role in determining salaries. On average, Sun Certified Java Programmers make approximately $78,000 a year while Sun Certified Developers make an average yearly salary of $84,500.

The first step in hiring a Java professional is determining the level of skill you require and preparing an incentive package. If your IT environment is mission-critical, then a seasoned Java programmer with at least 5 years of experience is your safest choice. Candidates, however, with high skill levels and many years of experience often require incentives to abandon their employers.

Preparing the Incentive Package

If you want a top-notch Senior Java Professional, you may be surprised to find them in short supply, even in a down job market. While every manager knows that salary alone cannot guarantee employee loyalty, there are a host of techniques used by IT management to attract and retain top-notch Java professionals.

Java professionals like the latest hardware and software!

In addition to a competitive salary, some of the techniques used to entice potential Java programmers include:

Flex time – Burnout can be a real problem among Java programmers who must typically work evenings, weekends, and holidays to stay current with many demanding and sometimes conflicting project tasks. Many companies offer formal comp-time policies or institute a four-day workweek, allowing the Java programmer to work four, 10-hour days per week.

Telecommuting – Many Java programmers are allowed to work at home and only visit the office once per week for important face-to-face meetings.

Golden handcuffs - Because a high base salary does not always reduce attrition, many IT managers use yearly bonuses to retain employees. Golden handcuffs may take the form of a Management by Objective (MBO) structure, whereby the Java programmer receives a substantial annual bonus for meeting management expectations. Some companies implement golden handcuffs by paying the employee a huge signing bonus (often up to $50,000) and requiring the employee to return the bonus if he or she leaves the company in less than three years. However, don't be surprised to find that some competing companies will reimburse the Java programmer to repay a retention bonus.

Fancy job titles - Because Java programmers command high salaries, many are given honorary job titles other than simply Java Programmer. These include Business Analyst, Programmer Analyst, Java Developer, and Systems Engineer. Other Java programmer titles include Vice President of Software Engineering, Chief Technologist, and the new job title (used by Bill Gates), Chief Software Architect.

Specialized training - Companies commonly reward Java programmers by sending them to conferences and training classes and an entire industry is built around these large Java events. For example, every year thousands of Java developers gather for one week in San Francisco for the JavaOne^{SM} conference. Here, great minds in Java get together to celebrate Java technology, innovation, community, and education. On June 10th 2003, Sun Microsystems also launched JavaOne Online for those wishing the JavaOne^{SM} conference could be held all year long. JavaOne Online was designed to portray the spirit of the physical JavaOne conference and offer it to Java developers worldwide. Other popular conferences among Java developers are:

- Software Development Conference and Expo

- Colorado Software Summit - Java™ and XML Programming Conference

- Conference on the Principles and Practice of Programming in Java™ in Kilkenny City, Ireland

- Premier European Developer Conference on Java™ Technology and Object-Oriented Software Engineering (JAOO).

- Gatherings offered by the Geek Cruise Line that combine technical conferences on hot topics like Java, Oracle, Perl with an ocean cruise. An Eastern Cruise called Java Jam 4 will be offered in January 2004.

Defining the Required Job Skills

A number of Java professionals mistakenly believe that the job of the Java programmer is purely technical. In reality, the Java professional must be efficient and knowledgeable in all areas of IT, because in many cases, he or she has the ultimate responsibility for overall design, implementation, and user acceptance of the final system. Because Java professionals are heavily involved in all phases of the software development lifecycle, they must have excellent interpersonal and communication abilities as well as technical skills.

Remember, knowledge of Java is not enough. An understanding of operating systems and computer-science theory is imperative as well. That is why employers like to hire Java professionals who also have a background in computer science, information systems, or business administration.

It's also critical to remember that Java certification tells employers only that the job candidate successfully passed a certification test on the technical aspects of the Java language. In the real world, Java certification is just one of many criteria used to evaluate a Java professional job candidate. Other criteria include the following:

Excellent Communication Skills - As one of the key stakeholders in any new systems development project, the Java programmer must possess exceptional communication skills. Effective communication skills not only include speaking but strong proficiencies in reading and writing as well.

In many application development shops, it is the responsibility of the programmer or developer to communicate technical and sometimes highly complex information to top-level management as well as other public groups. As the central technical guru, he or she must be able to explain concepts clearly in terms of the big picture. The audience may consist of all stakeholders including management, users, DBAs, and other programmers participating in strategic planning and architectural reviews.

Formal Education - Many employers require Java programmers to have a bachelor's degree in Computer Science or Information Systems. For advanced positions such as a Principle Software Architect or Enterprise Development Architect, many employers prefer a Master's degree in Computer Science or a Master's in Business Administration (MBA).

Real-World Experience - This requirement is the catch-22 for newbies who possess only a Sun Java Certification. A common complaint among those who have Java Certification but no job experience is that they cannot get experience without the certification, and they cannot get a job without experience. This is especially true in a tight job market.

Problem Solving Abilities - A successful candidate should also have the ability to translate raw concepts from vague design specs and paper-based storyboards, through prototypes, and all the way to a finished product. When analyzing problems in development, experienced Java programmers are able to recommend and implement effective solutions throughout all phases of development. They possess a deep-seated desire to develop innovative learning and teaching products and show profound capabilities for learning new topics. With excellent problem solving and organizational skills, a good candidate will possess the ability to evaluate information while making efficient architectural and design decisions.

Knowledge of Object-Oriented Design Theory - In addition to mastering the technical details required for the Sun Java Certification exams, the successful Java programmer must have an understanding of object-oriented design methodologies. This includes intimate knowledge of object-oriented design theory, object-oriented application design, CRC methods, design patterns as well as object-oriented modeling with Unified Modeling Language (UML).

💻 **Code Depot Username = reader, Password = coffee**

Basic IT Skills

Because the Java programmer is often called upon to participate in critical projects in the IT department, a broad background is often desirable. Much of this basic IT knowledge is taught in academic Computer Science and Information Technology programs. Non-Java programming job skills include:

System Analysis & Design - Many Java programmers must take an active role in analyzing and designing new application systems. Hence, knowledge of relational databases, data flow diagrams, CASE tools, entity-relation modeling, and design techniques enhance the Java professional's scope of ability.

Database Design - Depending on the application being designed, many Java programming jobs require knowledge of some database theory, STAR schema design, and data modeling techniques.

Data Security Principles - An understanding of database security, including role-based security, is useful, especially for US Government positions.

XML and Web Services - Knowledge of XML and Web Services (UDDI, SOAP, ebXML, WDSL) is essential when designing distributed enterprise systems.

Change Control Management - In many cases, the Java programmer will be responsible for utilizing version control and code sharing systems to ensure that changes to the production code base are properly coordinated. Knowledge of third-party change control tools, such as the UNIX Source Code Control System (SCCS), CVS, Oracle SCM, or Continuus is essential.

Now that we have an understanding of some of the required skills, let's talk about Java certification. The Sun Java Certified Professional exams identify candidates who have mastered specific technical areas within the Java programming language. However, as interviewers frequently discover, certification provides no guarantee that a candidate has real Java development expertise.

Sun Certified Java Programmers and Developers

Lured by the promise of a large paycheck, thousands of ordinary people from every walk of life have managed to complete "Java boot camps" that teach them how to pass the Sun Certified Java exams. Possessing only certification from Sun Microsystems as either a Java Programmer or a Java Developer, these individuals are applying for and obtaining jobs in application development shops without the appropriate IT background. If this is possible and happening in today's job market, then what is the value of certification in Java?

The Value of Java Certification

So, what is the value of Java Certification? Considering that Java Certification Exams cost $150 each and factoring in the cost of books, classes, and other study materials, Java certification is a sizable investment. However, the potential rewards can make that investment worthwhile.

Here's the catch - Java Certification alone is not a guarantee that anyone will find employment in application development. A Java Certification is just one of the credentials valued by prospective employers.

All together, there are five Java certifications offered by Sun Microsystems that are divided into two major technology areas: Java 2 Platform, Standard Edition (J2SE) and the Java 2 Platform, Enterprise Edition (J2EE). The following section provides a brief description of all five Java certifications within the J2SE and J2EE technology areas:

Java 2 Platform, Standard Edition (J2SE)

Sun Certified Programmer for the Java 2 Platform - This certification is for programmers interested in demonstrating proficiency in the fundamentals of the Java programming language, including Objects and Classes, Modifiers, Flow Control, Operators and Assignments, Exceptions, I/O, Collections and Maps, Inner Classes, Threads, and use of the `java.lang` and `java.util` packages.

Sun Certified Developer for Java 2 Platform - This certification is designed for programmers and developers who already understand the basic structure and syntax of the Java programming language. Candidates seeking this performance-based certification must demonstrate advanced proficiency in developing complex, production-level applications using J2SE. They should also possess strong skills in using Swing Components and Events, Layout Managers, Networking with Sockets and RMI, Threads with NIO and Swing, and working knowledge in Relational Database Technology utilizing JDBC.

Obtaining certification as a Sun Certified Developer consists of two elements: a programming assignment and an essay exam. Applicants must also hold Sun Certified Programmer for Java 2 Platform (any edition) status.

Java 2 Platform, Enterprise Edition (J2EE)

Sun Certified Web Component Developer for the Java 2 Platform, Enterprise Edition - This certification is for programmers developing Java web applications. Achieving this certification demands an in-depth knowledge of applications development, using JavaServer Pages (JSP) and servlet technologies to present Web services, and dynamic Web content using J2EE. Candidates with this certification should also have strong skills in servlet session management, Thread safety with servlets, web application security, and web application deployment, plus the ability to customize tag libraries and design patterns.

To be certified as a web component developer, individuals must pass one exam and also must possess Sun Certified Programmer for Java 2 Platform (any edition) status.

Sun Certified Business Component Developer for the Java 2 Platform, Enterprise Edition

- This certification was designed for Java developers who specialize in leveraging the J2EE platform-employing technologies used to develop server-side components that encapsulate an application's business logic. This certification concentrates on testing a candidate's knowledge of designing, coding, testing, deploying, and integrating Enterprise Java Beans (EJB) applications.

To be certified as a Business Component Developer for Java, individuals must pass one exam and also must possess Sun Certified Programmer for Java 2 Platform (any edition) status.

Sun Certified Enterprise Architect for the Java 2 Platform, Enterprise Edition

- This certification is intended for enterprise architects responsible for designing J2EE-compliant applications. It tests a candidate's skill sets in producing applications that are scalable, flexible, and highly secure. A candidate should be exceedingly familiar with resolving complex design issues and the technologies offered in the Java 2 Platform, Enterprise Edition, used to build Java-based enterprise applications

Obtaining a certification as an Enterprise Architect for Java consists of three elements: a knowledge-based multiple-choice exam, an assignment, and an essay exam.

Training for Certification

The Sun Java Certification program has evolved into a structured array of exams and certifications, and the number of exams will only continue to evolve as new functionality is added to the Java platform. The popularity in Java certification has created a new market for classes and books dedicated to helping candidates pass the exams. Although knowledge of the Java platform is enough to enable an individual to pass any of the exams, candidates often purchase books that contain practice exams. Often these practice exams provide the candidate with a general feel for the testing environment and whether or not they may be ready for the actual exam.

Both Java programmers and hiring managers can use certifications as a gauge of competence, but real-world experience must never be discounted. Certification in Java is not a complete measure of a person's skills. However, it does signify a modicum of talent and provides a method for those with degrees in Computer Science or Business Administration to enter the Java programming job field.

For a Java programmer candidate, depth of knowledge in object-oriented programming design, problem solving techniques, and years of experience is far more important than their ability to pass the Sun Certified Java exams. Employers are recognizing the pitfalls of hiring based solely on Java certification.

Characteristics of the Java Professional

Many application development shops have hundreds of technology workers. However, retention efforts are normally focused on seasoned Java professionals, whose knowledge of the company's application systems is not easily transferred to replacements.

In many development shops, the Java professional may fill many roles. In addition to the traditional responsibilities found in software engineering, the Java professional is often called upon to serve as a system architect, a database administrator, or a system administrator. He or she may also be asked to serve as an "informaticist" (a functional IT professional with an MS in computer science who is also trained in professional areas, such as medicine, business management, or accounting).

A first rate Java professional might possess the following attributes:

Has earned at least one professional degree or certification - Having a degree such as MD, JD, MBA, MSEE, or CPA, in addition to an undergraduate degree, makes an employee a valuable asset, and one difficult to replace in the open job market.

Has graduated from a competitive university - Java programmers must be self-starting and highly motivated to be effective. These qualities are often shared by those who've gained entrance into competitive universities with rigorous admission standards. These schools include most Ivy League schools, especially MIT, and universities with stellar reputations in Information Systems such as Purdue, the University of Texas, the University of California at Los Angeles, the University of San Diego, and the University of California at Berkeley.

Is trained in a special skill - Java programmers with specialized, difficult-to-find training are often in high demand. Such programmers have skills in areas such as ERP Systems (Oracle 11i, SAP, BaaN), Relational Database Technologies (Oracle, MySQL, PostGress), and J2EE Platforms (Oracle9iAS, BEA WebLogic, IBM WebSphere).

Active in the Java community - Many good Java programmers participate in local user groups, present techniques, and publish in many of the Java-related periodicals.

Is recognized as a Java expert - A sure sign of a top-notch Java professional is someone who comes to the forefront of audiences by publishing a book, writing a magazine article, or appearing as a conference speaker.

Possesses irreplaceable knowledge of an institution's enterprise systems - If the employee serves in a mission-critical role such as Chief Architect or Principal Software Engineer, that employee's departure may create a vacuum in the Application Development Department.

Sample Job Sheet for a Senior Java Enterprise Developer

Applicants for any Java professional job are expected to meet all the requirements in mission-critical areas, including education, experience, certification, writing credits, personal characteristics, and legal standing. Here is a sample Java programming job requirement sheet:

Sample Java Job Sheet

These are the minimum job requirements for the position of Senior Java Enterprise Developer. The HR department will pre-screen all candidates for the following job skills and experience.

Education

Persons should have a Bachelor's and a Master's Degree, preferably from an Ivy League institution. At a minimum, the candidate is expected to possess a four-year degree from a fully-accredited university in a discipline such as Computer Science, Software Engineering, or Engineering (electrical, mechanical, or chemical), or a BA or MBA in Information Systems (from an AACSB accredited university).

Work Experience

The candidate should have five or more years of programming experience in object-oriented Java, two or more years programming experience with the Java 2 Enterprise Edition platform, and three or more years experience programming in Unix/Linux system environments.

Sun Java Certification

The Java programming candidate must have earned a Sun Java Programmer Certification or Sun Java Developer Certification at some time in the last two years.

Publishing and Research

The candidate should show an active interest in publishing Java research by participating in user groups and publishing articles, books, and columns on the subject. These include:

Books. Submitting proposals for publication to Java technical books or any other recognized academic publication company.

Articles for academic journals. Publishing articles in academic journals such as the *Journal of the IEEE*, *Management Science*, *Journal of Management Information Systems* and the *Journal of Systems & Software*.

Conference papers. Writing papers and presenting at conferences such as Java World, JAOO, and Colorado Software Summit.

Articles in trade publications. Writing articles for a trade publication such as *Java Developer's Journal*, *JAVA Pro*, *Java World*, or *Dr. Dobbs Journal*.

Personal Integrity

This position requires designing and coding mission-critical applications and accessing confidential data, so all candidates are required to sign a waiver to disclose personal information.

The candidate must have no history of acts of moral turpitude, drug use, dishonesty, lying, cheating, or theft.

USA Citizenship

We are unable to sponsor H1-B foreign consultants. Therefore, candidates must provide proof of US citizenship or appropriate visa.

Additional Specialized Skills

The following specialized skills are desired:

- Bachelors or Masters Degree from a major university.

- Active US Secret, Top secret or Q-level security clearance.

- Working knowledge of Oracle9*i*AS Containers for J2EE (OC4J).

- Ability to use case design.

- Ability to work with human resource systems from Oracle11*i*, SAP, or PeopleSoft.

- Strong knowledge in UNIX scripting languages including KSH and BASH

Positions as a Java professional have requirements that vary widely, and it is up to the IT manager to choose those qualities most suitable for the position.

Conclusion

This chapter has been concerned with identifying the job requirements of a skilled and experienced Java programming candidate and in preparing an incentive package. Next, let's take a look at how to evaluate the Java programmer for specific job skills.

Successful Java Programmer Qualities

Determining the quality of a successful candidate starts with evaluating the résumé. This is a critical part of the selection process. In a tight job market, it is not uncommon for HR and IT management to receive hundreds of résumés. It is important that they understand how to fairly and efficiently pre-screen applicants and only forward qualified individuals to the hiring manager for an interview. Let's start by looking at techniques for assessing the job history of a Java programmer.

A good Java programmer will demonstrate persistence!

Evaluating Employment History

Without question, critical appraisal of a Java professional's work history is the single most important factor in résumé screening.

In most cases, candidates without a significant amount of work history will spend an excessive amount of time learning their jobs, while a higher-paid, experienced candidate may be a better overall value for the hiring company.

Not all Java programming experience is equal. Many demanding application development shops provide exceptional training and experience, while others provide only glancing exposure to the Java environment.

When evaluating the work experience of a Java professional candidate, the following factors should be considered:

Job role - Java programming candidates who have held positions of responsibility in areas that require design and architecture decisions are often more qualified than those candidates for whom Java programming skills were a part-time duty.

Employer-sponsored Java education - Within many large corporations, IT employees are encouraged and in some cases required to participate in annual training events to keep their skill sets current. One good indicator of how current an applicant's job skills are is how much on-the-job education is cited on his or her résumé. Employer-sponsored, yearly Java training and participation in Java groups and conferences (JavaOne[SM], JAOO) are indications of a good background for a Java professional.

Fraudulent Work History

In the soft market of the early twenty-first century, it is not uncommon for a desperate Java professional job seeker to forge a work history with a defunct dot-com. The desperate applicant hopes that this fraud will not be detected. This phenomenon presents the IT manager with a unique challenge in verifying employment history with a company that no longer exists or contacting job references who, perhaps, cannot even speak English.

In many cases, the HR staff tends to discount résumés with employment and educational history that cannot be completely verified. Many departments, frustrated with confirming overseas employment histories, never forward these types of résumés to the IT manager.

Evaluating Personal Integrity

It is always a good idea to perform a background check, which is easily obtained via national services. Many companies require that a candidate not have any criminal convictions, except minor traffic violations. In some cases, a routine background check can reveal arrests and acts of moral turpitude.

A Java professional's ongoing responsibilities often include designing and coding mission-critical applications with confidential data. Therefore, some companies require that all applicants for Java programmer or developer positions be expected to demonstrate the highest degree of personal and moral integrity.

In addition, background checks that reveal a history of drug use, dishonesty, lying, cheating, or theft may be grounds for immediate rejection. In some companies, all applicants are expected to sign a waiver to disclose personal information and are asked to submit to a polygraph exam.

Evaluating Academic History

While formal education is not always a predictor of success as a Java professional, there can be no doubt that job candidates with advanced degrees from respected universities possess both the intelligence and persistence needed to be a top-notch Java developer.

The Quality of Education

When evaluating the educational background of job candidates, it is important to remember that not all colleges are created equal. Many IT managers tend to select candidates from top tier colleges and universities because they rely on the universities to do the pre-screening for them.

For example, an IT professional who has been able to enroll in a top tier university clearly demonstrates high achievement, intelligence, and a very strong work ethic. At the other end of the spectrum, there are many IT candidates who have attended vocational schools, night schools, and non-accredited universities to receive bachelor's degrees in nontraditional study areas. In many cases, these IT professionals lack the necessary technical and communicational skills required to succeed in the IT industry.

The type of degree a candidate has attained is also a factor in how suitable he or she is for the position. For example, an ABS or MS in Computer Science generally requires the IT job candidate to have a very strong theoretical background in mathematics and physics. Those with formal degrees in computer science tend to gravitate toward software engineering and software development fields that require in-depth knowledge about lower-level components in computer systems.

On the other hand, BS and MBA degrees in Information Systems offered by accredited business colleges (accredited by the American Assembly of Collegiate Business Schools, AACBS) tend to strike a balance between IT programming skills and business skills. The information systems degree candidate will have a background in systems analysis and design, as well as familiarity with functional program development for specific business processes.

Unlike computer science majors, information systems majors will have a background in accounting, finance, marketing, economics, and other areas of business administration that equip them to solve business problems.

Many IT shops save time by letting universities pre-screen Java programmer candidates. For example, MIT carefully screens grades and achievement, and this allows companies to choose computer science professionals from MIT with increased confidence in the candidate's required skills.

The type of job to be filled may determine the academic history required. For example, a Java developer/programmer position may not require a four-year degree, while a lead Java analyst for a large corporation may require a Master's degree from a respected university.

Note: This section is based on the author's experience in evaluating Java programmers and the HR policies of large application development shops. This section is in no way meant to discredit those Java job applicants without the benefit of a college education.

Rating College Education

Many shops have an HR professional evaluate education, while other IT managers take it upon themselves to evaluate the technical quality of the Java professional candidate's formal education. Fortunately, sources for rating colleges and universities can be found online. Many large corporations require that the job candidate's degree must be from a university possessing a first-tier or second-tier rating by US News & World Report's "America's Best Colleges" or degrees from exceptional universities (as listed in the Gourman Report).

Of course, not all jobs as a Java professional require a college degree. For lower-level Java positions, the formal academic requirements are less stringent, but the lead Java developer for a large corporation must possess high intelligence, superb communications skills, and the drive and persistence that is most commonly associated with someone who has taken the time to invest in a quality education.

College Major and Job Suitability

There is a great deal of debate about what academic majors, if any, are the best indicators of future success as a Java programmer. However, it is well documented that different majors attract students with varying abilities. The following list describes some indicators used in large corporations for assessing the relative value of different college majors:

Engineers - Engineers tend to make great Java programmers, especially those with degrees in Electrical Engineering (EE). An engineering curriculum teaches logical thinking, algorithm design, and data structure theory that makes it easy for the engineer to quickly learn the concepts of object-oriented programming with Java. However, while engineers have unimpeachable technical skills, their oral and written communication skills are often lacking. Therefore, IT managers should pay careful attention to communication skills when interviewing Java applicants with engineering degrees.

Business Majors - Business majors make excellent Java programmers and analysts because of their training in finance, accounting, marketing, and other business processes. Many business schools also require matriculated students to take several courses in Information Technology. Of course, not all college business schools are equal. When evaluating a Java job seeker with a business major, screeners should ensure that the degree is from a business school accredited by the American Assembly of Collegiate Business Schools (AACBS). There are many tiers of business schools, offering vastly different levels of training.

Computer Science Majors - Computer scientists typically receive four years of extensive technical training, and are ideal candidates for the role of jobs requiring in-depth technical ability. However, like engineers, many computer scientists have less-desirable communications skills.

Music Majors - For many years, IBM recruited from the ranks of college musicians because hiring managers found that musicians possessed an ability in logical thinking that made them ideal candidates for IT skill training.

Math Majors - Math majors tend to possess excellent logical thinking skills and often possess a background in Computer Science. Like many quantitative majors, social and communications skills may be a concern.

Education Majors - Evaluation of education majors is extremely difficult because of the wide variation in quality between universities. Nationally, GRE test rankings by academic major show that education majors consistently rank in the lowest 25% of knowledge. Any applicant with an education major should be carefully screened for technical skills, and the college ranking checked in *US News & World Report's* "America's Best Colleges".

Some computer professionals are insecure about their vocabulary

International Degrees

A huge variation in quality exists among international degrees. Therefore, Java candidates with international degrees should be carefully checked in the Gourman Report of International Colleges and Universities.

Some sub-standard overseas colleges have no entrance requirements and require little effort from the student. There has also been a rash of résumé falsifications of college degrees from overseas colleges. The fraudulent applicant is often relying on the human resource department's inability to successfully contact the overseas school to verify the applicant's degree.

In sum, international degrees should be carefully scrutinized. It is recommended that, where appropriate, foreign language professionals are hired to write the letters to request verification of the graduate's attendance, and to obtain and translate the college transcript.

Advanced Degrees and Java Professionals

The percentage of Java professionals for large corporations possessing an advanced degree (Master's or Doctorate) is increasing. While an advanced degree shows dedication to a professional position, the quality of the degree is of paramount concern.

A higher ranking should be given to an on-site Master's degree from a respected university than to a night school or "non-traditional" graduate school. These non-traditional schools often have far lower acceptance standards for students and are far less academically demanding than the top US graduate programs.

The New Graduate

Regardless of the educational experience of the graduate, there will likely be little in the applicant's background that will prepare him/her for the real-world business environment. Computer curricula tend to emphasize theoretical issues of interest to academicians that may have little direct bearing on the needs of your shop.

The recent graduate may have grandiose visions of designing and maintaining whole software systems. They may be very adept at writing code from scratch, but will rarely be called upon to do this.

New College graduates are sometimes immature.

Instead, your company will need someone who can work within the existing software system without crashing and burning the place down. What's of major importance here is the ability to read OPC (Other People's Code). The candidate with the ability to slog through existing code and understand it is the candidate who will be able to add data and make changes in your production system without bringing operations to a grinding halt.

Moreover, the work that the new employee does on the software system will undoubtedly be modified and altered by others in the future, as new needs develop and hidden problem areas emerge. For this reason, a candidate who is able to show the technical interviewer that she has excellent documentation skills and habits can be much more of an asset to the company than someone who is not accustomed to submitting work that must be accessible to others. Several of the questions in Chapter 5 are useful in gauging these traits.

Personality of the Java Professional

What is more important to managers, technical knowledge or personality? Many times, managers concentrate too much on technical skill, and a candidate's personality is overlooked.

In almost every core job function mentioned previously, the Java professional's work comprises interacting with vendors, users, DBAs, managers, and even other developers. With that in mind, the following professional personality traits are, or ought to be, embodied by the successful Java professional.

Some Java programmers have split personalities.

These traits are important for people in almost any profession, but they are particularly important for the Java professional. Let it be said of the successful candidate that he or she is self-confident, curious, tenacious, polite, motivated, and a stickler for details.

For some Java programmers, everything is an emergency!

Self-confidence

Java professionals that lack self-confidence, ask the manager's opinion on every decision no matter how large or small, and show no initiative, are not all-star material. This indecision may be acceptable for an entry-level Java programmer being supervised by a senior Java professional, but the candidate should be expected to learn to depend on his or her own judgment for important decisions.

In interviews, questions must be asked about problems encountered and how the applicant would resolve the problems. Answers provided should reflect self-confidence.

A Curious Nature

Curiosity is a core trait of the Java professional because the Java platform is constantly changing, and it is sometimes difficult to find examples and documentation for those changes in the language. A Java professional who is not curious is passive and reactive, while a curious Java professional is proactive. The proactive Java professional will install the latest version of the Java platform and find enhancements that will make their code more efficient and easier to read, and in many cases, will improve performance.

Some Java programmers don't take initiative.

The curious Java professional invests personal money to stay current. In interviews with potential candidates, questions should be asked about the books and professional publications the candidate relies upon. Needless to say, answers indicating sole reliance on "the documentation set" are not an indication of professional curiosity.

Because curiosity is a requirement for a good Java professional, another set of interview questions should involve the Java APIs and the constant flow of new classes and packages provided in the Java platform. A top-flight Java professional is not lacking in awareness of the Java APIs and of the basic classes and packages provided by the latest Java specification.

A Tenacious Disposition

Like most disciplines in the IT industry, a Java programmer or developer requires bulldog-like tenacity for successful troubleshooting. The Java professional should enjoy knuckling down on a problem and not giving up until an answer is found.

In the *comp.lang.java* newsgroup, thousands of questions have been posted by Java professionals out in the field. Many times, the questions are about problems that would have been solved had the developer tenaciously pursued solving them rather than giving up.

Polite Manners

A Java professional works closely with other people. Therefore, tact is required when dealing with managers, users, DBAs, and even other developers.

Java programmers have a reputation for poor manners!

But here's a fact of life for developers or programmers: Project managers, DBAs, and users will bring forth unreasonable requests and impossible deadlines. The Java professional must cultivate interpersonal skills to respond to such requests without burning bridges. Ill-will is fostered outside the application development department by a rude programmer or developer. The Java professional must be extra polite, beginning in the job interview.

Self-Motivating

Employers recognize and value self-starting employees. These are employees who require little in the way of supervision and constant spoon-feeding. Much more in the way of self-motivation is expected from the Java programmer than other IT professionals; primarily because they are the ones that must take charge of critical architecture and design decisions to produce a successful system. In addition, successful Java professionals foresee and prevent problems early in the system design, and seasoned professionals know what can cause trouble if they are ignored.

Motivation is a major factor in successful Java programming.

A self-motivated Java professional will have a history of programming and debugging techniques that can be applied in making the most efficient use of his or her time during system development.

A self-aware Java jockey sees reality clearly.

In an interview, the successful Java professional is able to respond to questions about Java language fundamentals, application development, and application deployment by talking about the systems they designed and coded. Therefore, the interviewer can craft questions about specific techniques to identify candidates who have actually been involved in a project's critical design and architectural issues.

Attention to Detail

Being detail-oriented is perhaps the most important trait for a Java programmer. Like most IT professionals, Java programmers are often described as having an "anal" personality for their attention to detail, after Sigmund Freud's theory of anal-retentive personalities.

Attention to Detail is critical for Java debugging.

A good Java programmer should not have to be told to crosscheck details or to document quirks observed during the design or coding phases. A detail-oriented or systematic person is early for an appointment and brings a PDA or calendar to an interview. Questions asked by the detail-oriented person should reflect the research conducted about the potential new employer.

Conclusion

This chapter has been concerned with the specific criteria for evaluating work and academic history. Next, let's look at the roles of Java programmers and get more insights into the characteristics of a successful Java programmer.

Any Java programmer who is fluent in Klingon may have a personality disorder.

Roles for the Java Programmer

A good Java programming candidate is able to articulate a solid knowledge of techniques in all areas of Java development, including coding and design, software configuration management, testing and debugging, use of the Java API libraries, 3rd party code reuse, and code documentation using Javadoc. In addition, a successful Java programmer in any organization must possess above-average communication skills.

Nit-picky Java programmers document everything!

Java Programmer Job Roles

The job of a Java programmer means many things to many people. In many cases, the size of the employer will determine what is required from a Java programmer. In a small shop, their duties are much broader than in corporations with teams of programmers and developers dedicated to specific projects.

The functions of the Java programmer can also be determined by other factors, such as whether the employer is doing custom development. Are they utilizing third-party packages that require integration? Will the application be Web-based and if so, will it be part of an application framework that is J2EE compliant? The interviewee and the interviewer must be prepared to discuss and understand what is expected of the Java professional and his or her role within the company hierarchy.

When a project begins that involves Java application development, be assured that shortly after the kickoff, many talents within your IT department will be involved, including Java programming, developing, and analysis. Java professionals will be involved from the start, interviewing end users, gathering business requirements, helping set expectations, and mulling over technical design issues. While coding remains the most crucial responsibility of the Java professional, many application development shops include other functions as part of this job position. Here are some common job duties for both Java programmers and developers:

Produce Specifications - Work with end users and project managers to write specifications that meet client requirements for applications. The programmer/developer will then work with clients and other consultants to program and code applications according to those specifications.

Determine User Requirements - Gather and work with requirements. This often involves Use Cases, UML diagrams, ERD diagrams, and other prototypes. The candidate should understand that the Use Case document is probably the most important of the documenting requirements. It contains the "stories" of how the user will eventually be utilizing the system. It is important that the candidate demonstrate past success in working with customers in documenting Use Cases and ensuring that they are clearly understood throughout the project life cycle.

Test Application Functionality - Work with clients and other team members to test an application's functionality, performance, and load according to specifications. Is the candidate able to demonstrate success in automating tests, performing unit tests, or using a testing framework like JUnit? The candidate should also have the ability to communicate those results to the proper stakeholders (project managers, executive sponsors, and so on).

Provide Technical Expertise - Provide technical advice and expertise to other technical team members within a project on system architecture, design, and technology alternatives.

Serve as Vendor and End-user Liaison - Serve as the official company representative and contact point for any Java software/platform vendor(s) contacted for technical support. It is often incumbent upon the Java professional to ensure compliance with Java software vendor on license agreements for the company.

To sum up, a full-charge Java professional candidate is knowledgeable in installation, project life cycle and methodology, software configuration management, Java security, Java application tuning, troubleshooting, vendor relations, and how to design and code application systems.

Let's drill-down and review the basic knowledge areas for the Java professional candidate.

Installation

Because each platform is different, the successful Java candidate stays current regarding installation and updates on the particular Java/J2EE software platform against which a system is running. Staying current isn't easy. A Java professional accustomed to working under Windows NT may have trouble with a UNIX installation. Incorrect updates and invalid configurations performed on production machines can result in big trouble.

In interviews for a Java position, questions about installing and upgrading the Java software components systems are to be expected. The candidate should be prepared to discuss his or her platform and any modifications performed on the standard installation.

Project and Development Life Cycle Methodologies

Java candidates should have a basic understanding of project and development life cycle methodologies. The Java candidate should be able to speak about projects that he or she may have worked on that involved providing levels of detail to the project manager using some of the more common life cycle models. These models include the spiral model, waterfall model, evolutionary prototyping model, reusable software model, and thruways prototyping model.

Software Configuration Management

Any candidate for a Java programmer position should have a clear understanding of Software Configuration Management tools and concepts. Is the Java candidate familiar with the notion of check-out/check-in, branching, merging, version selection rules, work areas, and scopes of visibility?

Java Security

An applicant should also have a clear understanding of Java's security model, a fundamental skill set in building distributed and enterprise applications. Specifically, an understanding of how Java provides an interface (sometimes called the "Java Sandbox") between a Java application and operating system resources must be demonstrated. Knowledge of how a security manager's work in Java is vital to success in establishing effective security policies within an application is also a necessity.

Java Application Tuning

Yet another one of those skill sets that is often more art than science is application tuning. It is almost always a requirement that an application not only be designed to solve a particular business problem, but be able to perform given a certain set of metrics. This often involves negotiating with end users and setting up user agreements and benchmarking requirements.

A successful Java candidate should be able to bring forward and demonstrate tuning strategies they have used in the past that may or may not have worked. Was he or she ever called upon to investigate and resolve performance tuning issues at different levels of the application (i.e., the database, network, host operating system)?

Candidates should be prepared to discuss the pros and cons of Just-In-Time compilers, profiling tools, garbage collection, efficient use of looping, data structures, and algorithms, multithreading, and synchronization.

Troubleshooting

The flair for troubleshooting is a characteristic that is not common to all people. The art of troubleshooting requires an analytical and systematic approach, where the problem is laid out in discrete parts, and each is attacked in a methodical fashion until the problem can be resolved.

A good Java programmer is always available!

Troubleshooting sometimes requires the Java professional to admit he or she does not know something and must have the wherewithal to look for the answer. In responding to questions about troubleshooting, the Java professional candidate should be prepared to discuss real-life experiences. The best examples are those illustrating a lot of thought and multiple troubleshooting steps.

Communication Skills

Great technical skills are needed by the Java professional, but technical knowledge alone does not guarantee job success. As mentioned earlier, a Java programmer needs to be polite when dealing with team members, managers, vendors, and end users. Because a significant percentage of Java programmers' work requires interacting with others on multiple levels, they must be able to speak, think, and write clearly and concisely. A good Java programmer should strive to set the standard for quality oral and written communication skills.

An inventory of a Java programmer's communication skills starts with the professional résumé. Their résumé should be easy to read and reflect the candidate's publishing and speaking credits. Whether they were a keynote speaker at a national conference or merely presented a topic at a local user group, those experiences document the candidate's communication skills.

The interviewer should bring questions about job experiences that required the candidate to write documentation or procedures. It should be assumed that candidates with an advanced degree, such as a Master's or PhD, have well-developed writing skills, or they would not have reached that level of education. Candidates should be encouraged to bring to the interview their dissertations or other writing samples.

A successful Java professional absolutely must possess strong verbal communication skills. The ability to listen is just as important as the ability to speak clearly. Their daily routine will include listening to complaints and requests, processing that information, and providing responses and instructions.

Conclusion

In sum, the Java programmer must have a well-rounded skill set, and not just technical skills. Next, let's explore screening techniques for Java professionals and examine techniques and tools for verifying technical skill.

You can always tell a successful Java programmer.

Initial Screening

Be Prepared

Thorough preparation and attention to detail during the screening process can save significant amounts of money and resources as well as prevent potentially disastrous problems from ever occurring. Filling vacant positions is expensive, and a careful approach during the initial screening can reap tremendous dividends over time.

Be sure to screen for mental health issues!

In the opinion of many IT managers, an effective Java professional should have plenty of significant real-world experience to supplement technical knowledge. It has become trendy in the past few years to create sub-categories of job roles, such as Java Development Production and Java Production Support. However, in many large corporations, the Java professional is the respected technical guru who participates in all phases of system development, from the initial system analysis to the final physical implementation. Hence, the Java professional generally has significant experience in development and systems analysis.

Troubleshooting skills are essential for the Java programmer.

The High Cost of Attrition and Hiring Overhead

The IT industry suffers from one of the highest attrition rates of all professional jobs. This is due, in part, to the dynamic nature of technology. An individual may find himself grossly underpaid and decide to market his skills within a relatively short period of time. Someone else may experience a lack of challenge in a job that he or she has successfully performed for some time.

For example, an IT job candidate might enter a shop that needs a great deal of work done, only to stabilize the environment to the point that they are bored most of the time. The IT manager must try to distinguish between the "job hopper" and the individual who is changing jobs solely because of a personal need for more challenging work.

The cost of hiring varies by position and by geographic location, but is rarely less than $10,000 per employee. Filling higher end positions, such as Senior Java Enterprise Developer, can often exceed $50,000, as specialized headhunters are required to locate the candidate, and these headhunters commonly charge up to 50 percent of the candidate's first-year wages for a successful placement. There are also the fixed costs of performing background checks and credit checks, as well as HR overhead incurred in checking the individual's transcripts and other résumé information.

Choosing Viable Candidates

While reviewing hundreds of applications for a single job, the IT manager must quickly weed-out "posers" and job candidates who do not know their own limitations. To be efficient, the IT manager must quickly drill-down and identify the best three or four candidates to invite for an in-depth technical interview by an experienced Java programmer. Shops that do not have a current Java professional generally hire a Java consultant for this task.

Java programming consultants are commonly asked to help companies find the best Java programmers for a permanent position. Later on in this chapter, some of the questions used when evaluating Java programming candidates for corporate clients are shown.

"Yes, I know Java, J2EE and two other computer words."

Dealing with IT Headhunters

When seeking to fill a top-level IT position such as senior Java programmer, Java enterprise developer, or chief architect, it is not uncommon to employ IT headhunters. These IT headhunters can charge up to 50 percent of the IT job's base salary in return for a successful placement.

However, the aggressive nature of IT headhunters often does a disservice to the IT candidate, and puts the IT manager in a tenuous position. For example, it is not uncommon for the IT manager to receive résumés from two different sources for the same candidate, each represented by different head hunting firms. In cases like this, it is prudent to immediately remove that candidate from the prospective pool, in order to avoid the inevitable feuding between competing headhunter firms.

When dealing with headhunters, it's also important to get a guarantee that the IT employee will remain in the shop for a period of at least one year and to amortize the payments to the headhunter over that period. Those IT managers who fail to do this may find themselves spending up to $50,000 for a job candidate who quits within ninety days because he or she is not satisfied with their new job.

It's also important to remember to negotiate the rate with the headhunters. While they may typically command anywhere between 20 and 50 percent of the IT employee's first-year gross wages, these terms can indeed be negotiated prior to extending an offer to the IT candidate. In many cases, this works to the disadvantage of the IT candidate, especially when the headhunter refuses to negotiate the terms, thereby making another candidate more financially desirable for the position.

General Evaluation Criteria

Remember, all Java professionals are not created equal. They range from the entry-level Java programmer to a fully skilled, fire-breathing Java enterprise architect with extensive credentials. What level of Java professional does the company require? Consider what happens if such a fire-breathing Java professional is employed in a position that requires only code maintenance of several legacy systems. That individual will soon grow bored and find fertile application development projects elsewhere. On the other hand, hiring an entry-level Java programmer for a slot that requires tenacity, drive, initiative, and top-shelf troubleshooting skills is begging for disappointment.

Not all Java programmers have equal intelligence.

It is not easy to match the right candidate for a given job. Given the choice between someone who could write a Java Virtual Machine from scratch (but lacked certain personality skills) and a technically inexperienced Java programmer who demonstrates the personality traits mentioned above, the less experienced candidate is often the best choice.

The typical entry-level Java programmer usually has a good-looking résumé that is full of projects and jobs involving Java. However, the interviewer must subtract points if that work involved third-party Integrated Development Environments (IDEs) that were pre-installed and the programmer's main duties were simple code maintenance. When the candidate can't answer in-depth questions concerning the fundamentals of the Java language, the person is a "Java newbie" rather than a Java-level candidate.

High scores should be given to candidates who have direct knowledge of Java utilities, such as JUnit, Javadoc, policytool, and jdb. Extra points should be given to candidates who have knowledge of J2EE APIs, like JDBC, JNDI, and EJBs.

Networking skills may be desirable for a Java programmer.

A rule of thumb for hiring Java professionals is to avoid hiring an overqualified person who won't be happy in a job with minimal responsibilities. In a shop that utilizes a third-party Integrated Development Environment (IDE) and relies on pre-configured code generators, an entry-level Java programmer should be hired who can jump into gear whenever required to perform code maintenance.

On the other hand, if a high-powered Java professional is needed, an inexperienced Java programmer should not be hired, unless that individual clearly demonstrates the motivation for high-end learning and the desire to become a full-fledged Java professional.

Gleaning Demographics from the Candidate

With the advent of strict privacy laws in the United States, the IT manager must be careful never to ask any questions that are inappropriate or illegal. For example, asking the marital status, the number and age of the children, or the age of the applicant himself may make the IT manager vulnerable to age and sex discrimination lawsuits. Hence, the savvy IT manager should learn to ask appropriate questions that still reveal the information, while protecting the manager and the company from lawsuits.

Don't wind-up in court over an illegal interview question!

An IT manager certainly does not want to discriminate against a job applicant, but the demographic aspects nevertheless factor strongly into a hiring decision. For example, the female job applicant that has three children less than five years of age may not be appropriate for an IT position that requires long hours on evenings and weekends.

Another consideration is age of the applicant. If the IT manager works for a company that guarantees retirement where age plus years of service equals 70, then hiring a 60-year-old candidate would expose the company to paying that candidate a lifetime pension for only a few years of service.

Elderly Java programmers can add spice to the workplace!

Other important demographical information in our highly mobile society is the depth of connection the IT candidate has to the community. Those IT candidates who do not have extended family, close relatives, and long-term relationships in the community may be tempted to leave the position to seek more lucrative opportunities in other geographical areas.

Given that this information is critical to the hiring decision and at the same time inappropriate to ask directly, the savvy IT manager may ask somewhat ambiguous questions to get this information. For example, the manager may ask, "What do you do to relax"? This open-ended question will often prompt the candidate to talk about activities they engage in with their families and with the community.

Generally, the selection of a Java professional can be accomplished in the following phases:

- Initial screening of résumés by HR department (keyword scan)

- Non-technical screening by IT manager (telephone interview)

- In-depth technical assessment by senior Java professional

- On-site interview (check demeanor, personality, and attitude)

- Background check (verify employment, education, certification)

- Written job offer

Résumé Evaluation

As mentioned, it is not uncommon to receive hundreds of résumés for a particular Java job position. The goal of the IT manager (or HR department) is to filter through this mountain of résumés and identify the most-qualified candidates for the job interview.

The HR department typically performs a quick filtering through a large stack of résumés to narrow the candidates down to a select few, which are in turn presented to the IT manager.

Some résumés may contain anomalies that can reduce the time required for screening. These anomalies are known as "red flags," and indicate that the job candidate might not be appropriate for the position. Such indicators can quickly weed out dozens of candidates, eliminating the need for a more detailed analysis of the résumé, saving company resources.

Résumé Red Flags

There are several important things to look at when scanning a stack of résumés. The following are a short list used by many IT managers:

Unconventional résumé formatting and font - Occasionally, you may see a nice résumé that is done in a professional font, but with elaborate graphics, sometimes even including photographs and illustrations. In extreme cases, résumés have been known to arrive printed on pink paper scented with expensive perfumes.

Too much information in the résumé - Another red flag is a résumé that tends to specify a great deal of non-technical information. For example, the job candidate may go into great detail about their love of certain sports, hobbies, or religious and social activities. In many cases, these résumés indicate an individual for whom the IT profession is not a great priority.

Puffing insignificant achievements - It is not uncommon for low-end IT positions to attract job candidates who will exaggerate the importance of trivial training. For example, an

IT job candidate may proudly list on her résumé that she attended classes on how to use Windows e-mail in the work environment. Of course, trivia within an otherwise nice résumé too often indicates a lack of real technical skill, and the job candidate may be making an effort to obfuscate that fact by simply listing anything that they can think of.

Gaps in employment time - It's important to understand that the technically competent IT professional is always in demand and rarely has any gaps in their employment history. Sometimes, IT professionals misrepresent their work chronology in their résumés. For example, if they are laid off and are job seeking for 90 days, they may not list that 90-day gap of unemployment in order to make themselves seem more attractive. Of course, the start and end dates of each term of employment must be carefully checked by the HR department, and any false indication of this should be grounds for immediate removal from the candidate pool.

Poor grammar and sentence structure - Because the IT industry tends to focus more on technical than verbal skills, you may often find candidates with exceptional technical skills, but whose poor writing ability is apparent on their résumés. Short, choppy sentences, incorrect use of verbs, and misspellings can give you a very good idea of the candidate's ability to communicate effectively via e-mail. Remember, the résumé is a carefully crafted and reviewed document. If you find errors in this, you're likely to hire a candidate who lacks adequate written communication skills.

Short employment periods — Within the IT industry, it is very rare to be dismissed from a position in less than six months. Even the incompetent IT worker is generally given 90 days before they're put on probation and another 90 days before they are dismissed from the job. Hence, an immediate red flag would be any IT employee whose résumé indicates that they've worked with an employer for less than six months.

"Yes, I was an NCAA Basketball All-star"

Some job candidate may lie!

Evaluating Training

Scanning résumés involves evaluating for two factors: work history and academic qualifications. Here are some criteria that have been used by major corporations for résumé screening.

Java programming job candidates used to have only two sources for determining their knowledge: experience and/or Java training classes. Experience speaks for itself and can be judged as to depth and level of experience. However, any training is only as good as what the candidate puts into the training. Candidates might either gain much or comparatively little from the experience of instruction in Java, depending on whether they took their "will to learn" and curiosity with them to class.

As I have noted, Java certification (offered by Sun Microsystems) is one benchmark of a modicum of competence. Java exams test the candidate's knowledge in all areas of the professional skill set, from Java language fundamentals to architecting enterprise J2EE applications.

In order to pass, a candidate will, in almost all cases, need to have had actual experience as a Java programmer and will need to have knowledge from multiple Java references. The tests were developed by over a dozen highly skilled and experienced Java developers and have been certified against hundreds of Java candidates. While obtaining a Java certification from these exams is no absolute guarantee that a candidate is fully qualified, it can be used as an acid test to separate the wheat from the chaff.

"I've been programming in Java for 35 years."

Telephone Screening

After reviewing the available résumés, you will be in a position to select a pool of candidates for further telephone screening. The telephone interview is a useful tool for eliminating those candidates whose actual qualities may not quite match their glowing résumés, saving the time and expense of conducting on-site interviews.

The telephone interview may be either unscheduled or prearranged. In either case, the candidate will be less prepared than for the more formal on-site interview. It can quickly become apparent whether he or she is appropriate for the position.

The telephone is your best tool for pre-screening technical skills.

The unscheduled telephone screening is an opportunity to discover how well the candidate thinks on his feet, and provides insight into his unrehearsed thoughts and feelings. It can also indicate how well the candidate is organized, since the person who must repeatedly search for basic necessary materials and documents at home is unlikely to demonstrate superior efficiency in the work environment.

The interviewer should cover all pertinent areas, with the goal of confirming the qualifications present in the résumé. The candidate should be well informed about those topics that the résumé indicates are areas of proficiency.

The telephone interview will also reveal a great deal about non-technical qualifications. Is the candidate personable and articulate? How well does he or she listen?

From information and impressions gathered from the telephone screening, the IT manager will be able to confidently select the best-qualified candidates for an in-depth technical interview.

Technical Pre-Testing

The job interview questions in this text are deliberately intended to be presented orally. These questions are designed to elicit answers that should indicate a high degree of experience and skill with a specific technology (or a lack of it). Many IT managers will require the job candidate to take an in-depth technical examination.

The technical examination may be given over the Internet, using job-testing sites such as Brain Bench, or they may be paper and pencil tests administered to the candidate before the start of a detailed job interview.

There are important legal ramifications for using these testing methods. Many job candidates who are not selected for an important position may challenge both the scope and validity of the test itself. These challenges have been applied even to nationally known aptitude tests such as the SAT and LSAT exams; IT exams, and language tests such as C++, C#, and, you guessed it, Java. These tests may be especially prone to challenge by the disgruntled applicant.

While it is important to do a complete check of all the technical abilities of the IT candidate, it is very important that a manager never cite the failure of one of these exams as the reason for removal from the applicant pool. This is a common technique used by IT managers when they find a particular candidate's knowledge of the field to be insufficient.

For example, in filling a highly competitive IT vacancy, very small things may make the difference between employment or not. In any case, when rejecting a candidate, the IT manager should generally cite something intangible, such as that the individual's job skills do not completely meet the requirements for the position; or a more nebulous answer, such as that the candidate's interpersonal skills will not mesh with the team environment. Remember, specific citation of failure of any tangible IT testing metric may open your company to challenges and lawsuits.

Developing Questions for Interviews

Interview questions should be diligently researched, and the expected answers listed prior to the interview. When open-ended questions are used, the interviewer should have the level of knowledge required to judge the correctness of the answers given by the candidate.

You cannot always identify drug users

The questions should be broken into categories and each should be assigned a point value based on either a scale, such as from 0–5, or according to difficulty. Technically competent personnel should review interview questions for accuracy and applicability.

At the conclusion of the interview, evaluation of technical ability should be based on the results derived using these point values.

In addition, "open-ended" questions should be included, such as "describe the most challenging problem you have solved to date," or "name one item that you have developed (in Java) that you are most proud of". These open-ended questions are designed to allow the Java job candidate to articulate and demonstrate communications skills.

The IT Candidate's Demeanor

During the face-to-face interview, the IT manager can glean a great deal about the personality of the individual simply by observing his or her body language and listening to the candidate speak. In many cases, the IT manager may assess the interview candidate on non-technical criteria, especially the behavior of the candidate when asked pointed questions. Some of these factors regarding demeanor include:

Eye Contact - IT candidates who are unwilling or unable to maintain eye contact with the interviewer may not possess the interpersonal skills required to effectively communicate with end users and co-workers.

Fidgeting - IT candidates who are experiencing high anxiety during an interview may cross and uncross their legs, sit uncomfortably, or twiddle their hair while speaking with the IT manager. These involuntary signs of discomfort may indicate that the candidate does not function well in the stressful environment of a busy IT shop.

Diction - For those IT positions that require exceptional communication skills, such as working with the end-user community, you can get a very good idea of the abilities of the job candidates simply by listening to their responses. For example, careful IT professionals may demonstrate the "lawyer's pause" before answering the question. This pause, of about two seconds, often indicates that the job candidate is thinking carefully and formulating his response before speaking.

Job candidates who formulate their answers carefully can be especially useful in those positions for which the risk of damage from impulsive verbal statements, without considering the consequences of the statement, is high. You can also assess how articulate the job candidate is by the use of filler words such as "you know," inappropriate pauses, poor diction structure, poor choice of words, and a limited vocabulary.

"My long-term career goal?
Actually, I want to get your job."

Appropriate Appearance

A Java professional job candidate who doesn't take the time to
put the right foot forward by maintaining proper appearance
probably doesn't have the wherewithal to perform adequately on

the job. Clean, appropriate clothing and proper grooming show that the candidate is willing to make the effort to please the employer. Candidates who are sloppy in appearance and mannerisms will bring those characteristics to the job and to their interactions with other parts of the company.

Make sure your Java programmer understands proper dress codes.

Savvy Java professionals will adopt the dress of the executive and banking industry. This attire generally includes:

- Crisp white shirt
- Conservative tie
- Dark suit
- Dark leather shoes

Proper job interview attire is important.

We will take a closer look at the on-site interview in the next chapter.

Conducting the Background Check

As we have repeatedly noted, a candidate's references must always be rigorously checked. Previous employers should be spoken with, if possible, to learn about a candidate's past work history. Many people are good at interviewing, but won't necessarily function in the job.

Because of the explosive growth of the IT industry, fraudulent résumés have become increasingly common. Job candidates have been known to fabricate their college education and the scope of their work experience, smooth over gaps in their employment history, and exaggerate their job skills. In some cases, job skills may be exaggerated inadvertently, because the job candidate has only a brief exposure to a technology and does not understand their own limitations.

Therefore, it is very important for the HR department to perform a complete résumé check before forwarding any of these candidates for detailed interviews with the IT manager. These background checks may require the candidate's waiver signature for the release of all medical, criminal, and credit-related records.

The high rate of fraud found in résumé applications has spawned a new industry of private investigators that, for a fixed fee, will check national databases, revealing any criminal activity on the part of the job candidate, a history of bad credit, and other moral and demographic factors that may be relevant to their suitability for the position.

Making the Initial Job Offer

Once the IT manager has chosen the first candidate, it is common to make an offer based on nationwide studies of the average salaries within the geographical area. For example, IT workers in expensive, professional, urban areas, such as New York City, will earn twice as much as an IT professional with the same skills, working in a cheaper suburban or rural area.

If you decide to make an offer to a candidate, it is a good idea to ask them the salary amount they have in mind. If the candidate is the first to mention a number, the company is placed in an advantageous negotiating position.

If the candidate indicates he will be satisfied with an amount that is lower than you were prepared to offer, then you have arrived at the ideal hiring scenario. You have a candidate that you have already decided is desirable for the position, and they will take less money than you had anticipated paying them.

On the other hand, if the candidate has an unreasonably high expectation given his skill level and the market in your area, he may have an unrealistic view of the current business environment. This can indicate either that the candidate didn't do his homework or simple wishful thinking. You might point out that the range for this position is somewhat lower than he anticipates. You can then offer the amount you originally had in mind, and negotiate from there.

The knowledgeable IT manager will try to offer a candidate with an excellent set of IT skills a balance between the "going rate" and other intangible benefits, to make the job appealing. Other intangibles might include additional vacation time, flextime, telecommuting, and other perks designed to make the job more attractive to the candidates.

Of course, the IT manager may deliberately reduce the size of the initial offer if he anticipates that the candidate may negotiate for more. A highly desirable IT candidate may be courted by multiple companies and will often respond to the job offer with a counteroffer, citing other employers who are willing to pay more for the same skill set. When this happens, the IT manager may soon be faced with the dilemma of paying more than he or she had anticipated for the candidate, and may also question the candidate's motive in earning a high salary.

Conclusion

In sum, while the recession of 2002 has created a shakeout within the lower ranks of Java programmers, IT managers remain committed to retaining their top Java talent, and those Java programmers with specialized skills are still in high demand.

In today's highly volatile work environment, the average Java professional rarely stays with a single employer for a long period of time. Competition remains extremely strong for those Java superstars whose skill and background make them indispensable. While some attrition of Java professionals is inevitable, there are many techniques that savvy IT managers can use to retain their top talent.

At this point, you should be ready to invite the candidate for an on-site interview. Let's look at an approach to conducting a technical interview to access the candidate's level of technical Java knowledge.

The On-site Interview

CHAPTER 5

Skills Evaluation

During the on-site interview, the Java programmer needs to be evaluated for both technical skills and non-technical personality traits that will indicate whether the candidate can be successful in the work environment.

Now it's your turn to ask the tough questions!

The specific areas that you choose to emphasize in the interview will depend on the nature of the position. A system's architect who coordinates the efforts of several people will need a different skill set than someone who primarily works only on code maintenance. Choose questions that will highlight the specific skills you need and look for past experiences that demonstrate those abilities.

An effective Java programmer must be able to wear many hats. He must have the discipline to manage multiple and many times conflicting tasks, the interpersonal skills to communicate with team members and project managers, and most importantly, the technical skills in Java. This may include, but is not limited to, object-oriented programming techniques, accessing relational databases using JDBC, working with multiple Threads, GUI programming with Swing, and many other Java language fundamentals. Ask questions that demonstrate these abilities and look for experiences that show accomplishments in these areas.

Questions from the Candidate

Most books and articles neglect to discuss the questions that the candidate may ask the interviewer. This is unfortunate, because whether or not the candidate asks questions, and the character of those questions, can reveal a lot about his personality and suitability for the job.

After all, the serious candidate is evaluating the company just as you are evaluating him. If he is able to ask intelligent questions that are intended to assess how well his particular abilities and goals will integrate with the job, he is actually doing part of your job for you.

A certain amount of nervousness is to be expected in the interview process, but the passive candidate who appears reluctant or unable to answer interview questions, as if under cross-examination, can only raise suspicions about the reasons for that reticence. Contrast this person with the engaging candidate who doesn't answer so much as he conversationally responds, volunteering the pertinent information while interspersing his responses with questions of his own.

The candidate's questions should focus on the tasks and responsibilities he will encounter in performing the job. If the candidate takes the initiative in this way, facilitating the interview as you mutually explore whether the position is a good fit, chances are he will bring this same constructive approach to the work environment once you determine that he is, indeed, the best person for the job.

Beware of the candidate who only seems to be interested in his salary and the other perks that he will enjoy. There will be time to discuss money once you both decide that the alliance between you is promising. The thrust of the interview should be on the requirements of the position and whether the candidate is equipped to meet them.

Telephone Pre-interview Questions

At some point in the process, you will be faced with a number of high-quality résumés in your file. Committing to an on-site interview costs time and money for both parties. It is therefore important to consider some pre-interview checking. Performing a telephone interview to pre-screen geographically remote candidates can help in avoiding travel costs associated with an on-site interview. Also, you should ask to see their previous work or to contact a former employer. As long as you remain discrete, this is generally not going to be an issue.

The following 10 questions should help in determining the technical skill set of any Java candidate. The questions are simple enough that any qualified Java programmer should be able to answer them immediately. If a candidate has a hard time answering these questions, they may not be appropriate for a full-time position as a Java programmer or developer.

1. What is the name of the class that is the super class for every class?

   Answer: Object

2. Is it possible to extend the `java.lang.String` class? Why or why not?

   Answer: No. `java.lang.String` is declared as final. A class declared as final cannot be used as a parent class in inheritance

3. What primitives are defined in Java?

   Answer: The primitive types defined in Java are: int, short, long, float, double, byte, char, and Boolean.

4. How are the methods `this()` and `super()` used within constructors?

   Answer: `this()` is used to invoke a constructor of the same class.

   Answer: `super()` is used to invoke a superclass constructor.

5. What is the difference between a static and non-static method?

   Answer: A static method is associated with the class as a whole rather than with specific instances of a class. Non-static methods can only be called through an object instance.

Answer: When using a static method, there is no need to create an object of that class to use that method. You can directly call that method on that class. For example, say class A has static function `f()`, then you can call `f()` function as A.`f()`. There is no need to create an object of class A.

6. In Java, what is meant by the phrase, "Write once and run anywhere"?

    Answer: Java is a multi-platform language. The idea is that a Java application can be compiled once and run on any platform, and the same results will be obtained. Java source code is compiled into bytecode, which is the intermediate language between source code and machine code. Java bytecode is not platform-specific, so it can be fed to any platform. The bytecode is fed to a Java Virtual Machine (JVM) for the platform on which it is running. JVMs exist for all major platforms, including MS Windows, Linux, Solaris, HP-UX, and even Macintosh. After being fed to the JVM, which is specific to a particular operating system, the platform-specific machine code is generated, thus making Java platform independent.

7. The Java language does not natively support multiple inheritances. What feature of Java can be used to simulate multiple inheritances in Java?

    Answer: Many of the benefits of multiple inheritances can be gained through the use of an interface. While Java only allows you to extend from one class, it allows you to extend one or more interfaces. Interfaces have to have all abstract methods (unlike abstract classes that can have some concrete methods). A class can implement a number of interfaces, thus giving a sort of multiple inheritances.

---

8. What is the difference between a constructor and a method?

Answer: A constructor is a member function of a class that is used to create objects of that class. Every class in Java has at least one constructor — whether is it implicitly or explicitly defined. It has the same name as the class itself, has no return type, and is invoked using the new operator. The purpose of a constructor is to perform any necessary initialization for the new object.

Answer: A method is an ordinary member function defined in a class. It is java code that has its own name, a return type (which may be void), and is invoked using the dot operator. Methods are used to operate on and manipulate the data within a class. Methods define what and how actions are performed on the data — they do things and they change fields.

9. What is the difference between an interface and an abstract class in Java?

Answer: A class in Java must be declared as an abstract class if it contains one or more abstract methods. An abstract method can be thought of as a prototype method – it is a method that contains no body. It is nothing more than a signature method followed by a semicolon. The only way to use an abstract method is to subclass it and implement all of its abstract methods. An abstract class can contain non-abstract methods and ordinary variable declarations. Keep in mind that not all methods in an abstract class have to be implemented in a single subclass. It is possible to subclass an abstract class without implementing all of its abstract methods, but the superclass MUST be declared as abstract.

Answer: An interface contains only abstract methods. It can declare constants but cannot implement default behavior for any of its methods. When you want to use an interface, you must "implement" it using the implements keyword. When you implement an interface, you must provide an implementation for all abstract methods.

10. What is the purpose of garbage collection in Java, and when is it used?

Answer: The purpose of garbage collection is to identify and discard objects that are no longer needed (or referenced) by a program so that their resources can be reclaimed and reused. A Java object is subject to garbage collection when it becomes unreachable to the program in which it is used. The Java interpreter keeps track of what objects and arrays have been allocated and can therefore determine when an allocated object is no longer referenced by any other object or variable. The garbage collector then knows it is safe to destroy the object, and does so.

Technical Questions

The following questions were developed in case no one in your organization is qualified to assess the job candidate's skill set. Even without detailed knowledge of Java, you can get some idea of the technical skills of your Java programming job candidate.

While this quick technical check can be administered over the telephone, it is often performed on-site by a Sun Certified Java Professional. Each question is designed to be unambiguous, with a clear and accurate answer.

The interviewer should begin by apologizing for asking pointed technical questions before reading each question verbatim. If a candidate asks for clarification or says that he or she does not understand the question, the interviewer re-reads the question. If the candidate fails to answer a question or answers incorrectly, the interviewer should respond "OK," and move immediately to the next question.

Important Note

The intention of this section is not to provide a comprehensive technical exam, and the technical questions in this chapter and the code depot are only intended to be examples. The only way to accurately evaluate the technical skills of a job applicant is to employ the services of an experienced person and conduct an in-depth technical interview and skills assessment.

Also note that the expected answers from the questions are highly dependent upon the version of the product and the canbdidates interpretation of the question. We have tried to make the questions as version neutral as possible, but each new release of every product brings hundreds of changes and new features, and these example questions may not be appropriate for your version. An experienced technical person should always administer the interview questions presented in this book.

Qualifications

1. Do you have any Certifications? (i.e. Java Programmer/Developer, Cisco, Microsoft, Oracle)

    Candidates _____

    Answer: _____

    Interviewers _____

    Comment: _____

2. Highest level of education?

    Answer: Most candidates in this field require a college education, preferably a BS in computer science, computer information technology, or related engineering field.

    Candidates _____

    Answer: _____

    Interviewers _____

    Comment: _____

Object-Oriented Programming Concepts

1. What is an Object?

    Skill Level: Low

    Expected answer: Understanding the concept of an object is paramount to grasping object-oriented programming in Java. The candidate should be able to convey three important concepts when describing an object:

    - An object is not the same as a class. Classes are the blueprints for a part of an application that defines methods and variables. Objects are the individual incarnations of the class, sometimes called *instances of a class*. Two instances (objects) of the same class may contain different data, but will always have the same methods (behavior).

    - Objects are used in Java to bundle both variables (attributes) and methods (behavior) together into a single entity. Variables are used to hold the state of an object. For a person object, this may include the person's age, height, weight, and so on. Methods are Java functions that define the behavior of the object and what the object is allowed to do, such as changing height, weight, or birth date.

    - Object-oriented technologies provide programmers and software developers many benefits. When using an object-oriented programming language like Java, you use abstract entities (software objects) to model objects you find in everyday life. These real-world objects share two characteristics: they all have *state* and they all have *behavior*. For example, a program might use software objects to model real-world bank accounts, automobiles, employees, or even a window on your computer.

Score: _____

Notes: _____

_____

2. What are the two things that make up an object in Java?

Skill Level: Low

Expected answer: Its attributes (variables) and behavior (methods).

Score: _____

Notes: _____

_____

3. What is a Class?

Skill Level: Low

Expected answer: When defining a class, ensure that the candidate does not use the terms "class" and "object" interchangeably. A class is a blueprint, or prototype, that lists all methods and variables that go into defining or constructing attributes common to all objects of a certain kind. Just like a blueprint, a Java class has exact specifications that will define its state and it behavior. The definition of a class is writing to a file with a `.class` extension. Consider creating an employee class. After creating the employee class, you must instantiate it (create an instance of it) before you can use it. When you create an instance of a class, you are actually creating an object of that type, and the Java Virtual Machine (JVM) allocates memory for the instance variables declared by the class.

4. What is an abstract method?

Skill Level: Intermediate

Expected answer: An abstract method is a method defined in an *abstract class* that has no code associated with it. Its purpose is to serve as a placeholder, indicating that subclasses must have a concrete implementation for it. Abstract methods are created by labeling it with the keyword `abstract`.

5. What is an abstract class?

Skill Level: Intermediate

Expected answer: A class in Java must be declared as an abstract class if it contains one or more abstract methods. An abstract method can be thought of as a prototype method — it is a method that contains no body, nothing more than a signature method followed by a semicolon. The only way to use an abstract method is to subclass it and implement all of its abstract methods. One thing about an abstract class is that it can contain non-abstract methods and ordinary variable declarations. Keep in mind that not all methods in an abstract class have to be implemented in a single subclass. It is possible to subclass an abstract class without implementing all of its abstract methods, but the superclass MUST be declared as abstract.

Score: _____

Notes: _____

_____

6. What is a Message?

Skill Level: Intermediate

Expected answer: Objects communicate with one another by sending messages to each other. Consider two objects: Obj1 and Obj2; if Obj1 wants Obj2 to perform one of its methods, Obj1 will send a *message* to Obj2.

There are times when the receiving object needs certain information before it can perform the actions of one of its methods. In this case, Obj1 would send the required information to Obj2 in the form of parameters.

The three components that comprise a message are:

- The object that is being addressed
- The method being called
- Any parameters required by the method

Keep in mind that messages can be sent and received to objects in a different process. (e.g., RMI)

Score: _____

Notes: _____

_____

7. What is encapsulation?

Skill Level: Intermediate

Expected answer: Encapsulation is a technique used to control access to members of a class. Object-oriented programming languages, including Java, provide the ability for one object to choose whether or not to expose its variables to other objects and allow them to inspect and even modify its variables. An object can also choose to hide methods from other objects, forbidding those objects from invoking its methods. Using encapsulation techniques, an object has complete control over whether other objects can access its variables and methods, even going as far as saying which other objects have access.

Score: _____

Notes: _____

_____

8. What are the benefits of encapsulation?

Skill Level: Intermediate

Expected answer: There are two major benefits in encapsulating related variables and methods into a convenient software bundle. The first is *modularity*. This allows the developer to write and maintain source code for one object independent of source code for another object. The primary benefit of modularity is that objects can be effortlessly passed around in a system, providing developers with the capability to share objects with expected behaviors. The second benefit of encapsulation is *information hiding*. This allows the developer to write classes with public interfaces that allow other objects to communicate with it. But the object can also maintain private information that is not accessible from other objects. This allows internal (private) methods to be changed without affecting other objects that depend on it. The ability to properly use your object does not depend on knowing the internals of how your object works in order.

Score: _____

Notes: _____

_____

9. What is Inheritance?

Skill Level: Intermediate

Expected answer: Inheritance is a mechanism that enables one class to inherit both the behavior (methods) and the attributes (variables) of another class.

The term "base class" is used to describe the class used as a basis for inheritance. Other terms used to describe the base class are "superclass" and "parent class".

The term, "derived class" is sometimes used to describe a class that inherits from a base class. Other terms used are "subclass" and "child class".

The extended class has all the features of the base class, plus some additional ones. Consider, for example, a student class that is derived from a more general people class. Fields called salary and jobPosition, which the people class lacked, can be added to the Student class.

By using inheritance, developers can add features to an already existing class; this is considered an important aid when designing a program that has many related classes. Using inheritance makes it easy for developers to reuse classes, which is a key benefit of object-oriented programming design.

Score: _____

Notes: _____

_____

10. What is Polymorphism?

Skill Level: High

Expected answer: Polymorphism lets an application decide at runtime, every time an operation is called, which of several identically named methods to invoke. Polymorphism, sometimes referred to as dynamic binding, late binding, or run-time binding, is a property of Java (and other object-oriented software) by which an abstract operation may be performed in different ways in different classes. It primarily deals with type hierarchies. In order for polymorphism to work, these different classes must be derived from the same base class. When using polymorphism in practice, the developer will involve a method call that actually executes different methods for objects of different classes. This allows developers to write code that does not depend on specific types, thus simplifying and clarifying program design and coding.

Score: _____

Notes: _____

_____

11. What are virtual functions and are they supported in Java?

Skill Level: High

Expected answer: Yes, virtual functions are supported in Java. In fact, Java class functions are virtual by default. A virtual function is a member function that is expected to be redefined in a derived class. When referring to a derived class object using an object reference to the base class, you can call a virtual function for that object and execute the derived class's version of the function. Within Java, the programmer does not need to declare a method as virtual. As stated earlier, this is the default behavior in Java.

In working with a non-object-oriented language, when the compiler comes across a function (or procedure), it determines precisely what target code should be called, and builds the machine language to represent that function call. In an object-oriented language like Java, this is not possible. The correct code to invoke is determined based on the class of the object being used to make the call, not the type of the variable. The byte code is generated so that the decision of which method to invoke is made at runtime.

Virtual functions enable runtime binding of function calls to the actual function implementation. From a technical perspective, virtual functions are functions of subclasses that can be invoked from a reference to their superclass.

Score: _____

Notes: _____

_____

12. What is runtime binding?

   Skill Level: High

   Expected answer: Within the context of Java, runtime binding means that the resolution of a function call occurs at runtime. This means that, when calling a (virtual) function, the call is not resolved by the JVM until runtime.

   Score: _____

   Notes: _____

   _____

13. In Java, how can you make a function without making it a virtual function?

   Skill Level: High

   Expected answer: Declare the method as `final`.

   Score: _____

   Notes: _____

   _____

Java Programming and Development

1. How many public classes are permitted within a single Java class file?

   Skill Level: Low

   Expected answer: You can only define one public class within a single Java class file.

   Score: _____

   Notes: _____

   _____

2. How many package statements (declarations) are allowed in a Java source file?

   Skill Level: Low

   Expected answer: Only one.

   Score: _____

   Notes: _____

   _____

3. Is it necessary to have a package statement in a Java source file?

   Skill Level: Low

   Expected answer: No.

   Score: _____

   Notes: _____

   _____

4. In a Java source file, which statement needs to come first, import or package?

Skill Level: Low

Expected answer: The package statement must come before any import statements.

Score: _____

Notes: _____

_____

5. If all three statement elements of a Java source file are included (imports, classes, packages), in which order must they appear?

Skill Level: Low

Expected answer: Package declaration, imports, and then all classes.

Score: _____

Notes: _____

_____

6. Consider a program that imports a large number of classes. Is there any performance degradation from importing many classes at runtime?

Skill Level: Low

Expected answer: No. The import statements only provide the compiler with class name abbreviations and have no performance impact at runtime.

Score: _____

Notes: _____

_____

7. What is the command-line utility used to compile Java source code into bytecode?

    Skill Level: Low

    Expected answer: The command-line utility is `javac`.

    Score: _____

    Notes: _____

    _____

8. What is the name of the method the JVM uses as the normal entry point for a Java application? What is its signature?

    Skill Level: Low

    Expected answer: The name of the method is `main()`. The signature for `main()` is:

    ```
    public static void main(String[] args)
    ```

    Score: _____

    Notes: _____

    _____

9. Is it a requirement that the `main()` method be declared as static? Explain why or why not?

    Skill Level: Low

    Expected answer: Yes, it is a requirement that the `main()` method be declared static. This is necessary so it can be invoked without having to construct an instance of the corresponding class.

    Score: _____

    Notes: _____

    _____

10. What are the four signed integral data types in Java? What are their sizes and range of values?

Skill Level: Low

Expected answer:

Data Type	Size	Minimum	Maximum
Byte	8 bits	-2^7	$-2^7 - 1$
Short	16 bits	-2^{15}	$-2^{15} - 1$
Int	32 bits	-2^{31}	$-2^{31} - 1$
Long	64 bits	-2^{63}	$-2^{63} - 1$

Score: _____

Notes: _____

_____

11. Within your Java application, you catch all exceptions and want to know the exact circumstances under which it occurred. Which method would you use from the `throwable` class to obtain a complete stack trace?

Skill Level: Low

Expected answer: You can get a stack trace from any exception object with the `printStackTrace()` method in the `throwable` class.

Score: _____

Notes: _____

_____

12. What is the difference between `System.out.println()` and `System.out.print()`?

Skill Level: Low

Expected answer: The `println()` method is used to display a line of text that ends with a newline character. The newline character causes the next line of text to begin displaying at the left-most edge of the next line, similar to the carriage return key on a manual typewriter. The `print()` method, on the other hand, does not add the newline character to the end of the line. This allows you to use several `print()` statements to display information on the same line.

Score: _____

Notes: _____

_____

13. When creating a `String` object, is it necessary to use the `new` operator?

Skill Level: Low

Expected answer: No. Java does not require you to use the new operator when constructing a new `String` object. In fact, it is more efficient than explicitly calling the constructor.

Score: _____

Notes: _____

_____

14. What is the value at which a String is automatically initialized?

Skill Level: Low

Expected answer: `null`.

Score: _____

Notes: _____

_____

15. How do you make a variable a constant?

Skill Level: Low

Expected answer: Declare the variable using the `final` keyword.

Score: _____

Notes: _____

_____

16. What does putting the + operator between two strings do?

Skill Level: Low

Expected answer: It concatenates the two strings together.

Score: _____

Notes: _____

_____

17. What characters can be legally used as the first character of a Java identifier?

Skill Level: Low

Expected answer: Any letter, the dollar sign ($), or an underscore.

Score: _____

Notes: _____

_____

18. What statement would you use to convert the String `str1` to an integer named `int1`?

Skill Level: Low

Expected answer:

```
int int1 = Integer.parseInt(str1);
```

Score: _____

Notes: _____

_____

19. What statement would you use to convert the String `str1` to a byte named `byte1`?

Skill Level: Low

Expected answer:

```
byte byte1 = Byte.parseByte(str1);
```

Score: _____

Notes: _____

_____

20. What statement would you use to convert the String `str1` to a long named `long1`?

Skill Level: Low

Expected answer:

```
long long1 = Long.parseLong(str1);
```

Score: _____

Notes: _____

_____

21. Which method of the `String` class is used to compare two strings while ignoring their cases?

Skill Level: Low

Expected answer: `equalsIgnoreCase()`

Score: _____

Notes: _____

_____

22. How many Boolean literals (values) are possible and what are they?

Skill Level: Low

Expected answer: There are two Boolean literals, `true` and `false`.

Score: _____

Notes: _____

_____

23. What is the name of the access modifier when you do not explicitly specify private, public or protected?

Skill Level: Low

Expected answer: The name is `default`.

Score: _____

Notes: _____

_____

24. What is an object wrapper?

Skill Level: Low

Expected answer: An object wrapper is a set of Java classes that are used to change basic data types (primitives) such as `int` or `float` into objects. For example:

```
char    -> java.lang.Char
short   -> java.lang.Short
int     -> java.lang.Integer
long    -> java.lang.Long
```

These object wrapper classes allow primitive data types to be passed polymorphically. They also contain methods to convert to and from strings.

Score: _____

Notes: _____

_____

25. What keyword is used in Java that allows you to develop a class that inherits from another class?

Skill Level: Low

Expected answer: The keyword is `extends`.

For example, to create a class `student` that extends class `person`, use:

```
class student extends person {
...
}
```

Score: _____

Notes: _____

_____

26. Is `int` an object in Java?

Skill Level: Low

Expected answer: No, `int` is a primitive data type in Java. If you need an integer object, use the object wrapper `Integer`.

Score: _____

Notes: _____

_____

27. Briefly describe the purpose of the Java Virtual Machine?

Skill Level: Low

Expected answer: The Java Virtual Machine, or JVM, is the term used for the Java interpreter. The JVM is an application used to run Java programs by interpreting the intermediate bytecode format of the Java programming language. Java source code is compiled into a binary `.class` file that contains the bytecode to be used by the JVM.

Score: _____

Notes: _____

_____

28. All command-line arguments being passed into a Java application are passed in as an array of Strings. What would you need to do if your application must have an integer value passed in? What, if anything, could go wrong while attempting this?

Skill Level: Low

Expected answer: If your program needs to support a numeric (for example, an integer) command-line argument, it must convert a String argument that represents a number, such as "14," to an integer. Here's a code snippet that converts a command-line argument to an `int`:

```
int arg1;
if (args.length > 0) {
arg1 = Integer.parseInt(args[0]);
}
```

The `parseInt` throws a `NumberFormatException` if the format of `args[0]` isn't valid. All of the number classes — integer, float, double, and so on — have `parseXXX` methods that convert a String representing a number to an object of their type.

Score: _____

Notes: _____

_____

29. How do you determine the `length` of a string in Java?

Skill Level: Low

Expected answer: Use the `length()` method of the String class. For example, the following code snippet assigns `nameLength`, an integer variable, equal to 11:

```
String fullName = "Alex Hunter";
int nameLength = fullName.length();
```

Score: _____

Notes: _____

_____

30. When a method is not meant to return a value, what keyword in Java should be used in place of the return type?

Skill Level: Low

Expected answer: The keyword that should be used is void.

Score: _____

Notes: _____

_____

31. What is a JAR file?

Skill Level: Low

Expected answer: The acronym JAR stands for Java Archive. It is a file format based on the popular .ZIP file format that is used to collect a group of many files into one. As for everything else in Java, JAR files are meant to be platform independent.

JAR files come in handy when you need to work on the Internet. Without the ability of a compressed JAR file, Web browsers were required to make repeated requests to a Web server to download all the files that make up an applet. Now, only one request has to be made to download this compressed file.

Also helpful is the fact that each entry in a JAR file can be digitally signed for security purposes.

JAR files can be created programmatically or through a command-line utility.

Score: _____

Notes: _____

_____

32. Are JAR files meant to be platform independent?

Skill Level: Low

Expected answer: Yes. JAR files are based on the popular .ZIP file format and are cross-platform so developers do not have to worry about platform issues.

Score: _____

Notes: _____

_____

33. Why is it important to override the `equals()` method in the Object class when using it to compare objects?

Skill Level: Low

Expected answer: The default implementation of the `Object.equals()` method when comparing two objects is to compare their memory addresses. If the two memory locations are the same, a true is returned from `equals()`; otherwise, false is returned. In almost all cases, this is not the criteria you to use to determine whether two objects are equivalent. You should override the `equals()` method with Java code that performs the tests appropriate for your situation to determines whether two objects are equal.

Score: _____

Notes: _____

_____

34. What is the package concept and use of packages?

Skill Level: Low

Expected answer: As you become more familiar with Java and start writing more code, it will become apparent that it is important to organize your Java code. You will start to notice that some of your Java classes are related in some way, and yet you will also find it hard to locate pieces of code that may be scattered throughout different files in different directories. Another common problem is Java classes with the same name. This really becomes apparent when attempting to reuse Java code on the Internet. Java provides a solution called a "package" to enable you to organize your classes into logical groups.

When you create a class, it is likely you will want to take advantage of the Java package solution to better organize your code. First, organize your related classes in a hierarchal directory structure on your file system. Next, edit the Java source code of all files and indicate to them what package they are in by adding the following statement at the beginning of each source file:

```
package <package.name>
```

Score: _____

Notes: _____

_____

35. Suppose you have a package named `com.acme` and you want to import all classes within this package into your application. Which import statement would you include in your Java application?

Skill Level: Low

Expected answer:

```
import com.acme.*;
```

36. When using the wildcard character "*" in an import statement, as in `import com.acme.*`, what should be included, and what should not be included?

Skill Level: Low

Expected answer: All classes located in the package `com.acme` should be included. Keep in mind, however, that the import statement does not work recursively, so it will not include classes beyond `com.acme` as in `com.acme.utils.classes`.

37. What is the difference between Java and Java 2?

Skill Level: Low

Expected answer: Java 2 is nothing more than another name for JRE/SDK 1.2 or higher. Sun made many sweeping changes between JDK 1.1 and SDK 1.2, mainly in its libraries and with the addition of collection classes. Also included in Java 2 were the extensions mechanism and the enhancement of Java's security policy.

38. What method in the `String` class is used to return a new string that is all uppercase?

Skill Level: Low

Expected answer: The method used is `toUpperCase()`.

Score: _____

Notes: _____

_____

39. What does the term "initialization" mean?

Skill Level: Low

Expected answer: "Initialization" refers to giving a variable an initial value when setting it up. Simply put, when you create a variable and assign it a value, you are said to be initializing the variable.

Score: _____

Notes: _____

_____

40. What exactly does the `trim()` method do?

Skill Level: Low

Expected answer: The `trim()` method is used to remove leading and trailing whitespace from a String (whitespace characters include carriage return, newline, spaces, and tabs).

Score: _____

Notes: _____

_____

41. Is it possible to cast a double value to a byte?

    Skill Level: Low

    Expected answer: Yes.

    Score: _____

    Notes: _____

    _____

42. Does a class inherit the constructors of its superclasses?

    Skill Level: Low

    Expected answer: No, a class does not inherit any of the constructors from any of its superclasses.

    Score: _____

    Notes: _____

    _____

43. Is it possible for an anonymous class to be defined as implementing an interface or extending a class?

    Skill Level: Intermediate

    Expected answer: An anonymous class can implement an interface or extend a superclass, but cannot be declared to do both.

    Score: _____

    Notes: _____

    _____

44. When overriding the `equals()` method of the `Object` class, which other method in the `Object` class should you override?

Skill Level: Intermediate

Expected answer: You should also override `haschCode()`.

Score: _____

Notes: _____

_____

45. Is it legal to declare a class to be a final abstract? Explain why or why not.

Skill Level: Intermediate

Expected answer: You cannot declare an abstract final class. The compiler will not allow you compile this as the modifiers (final and abstract) indicate totally conflicting inheritance functionality for the class on which they are used.

The final keyword when used with regards to a class means that the class cannot be extended. (i.e., java.lang.String is an example of a class that cannot be used as a parent class in inheritance)

The abstract keyword when used with regards to a class indicates that the class cannot be instantiated, and instead is designed for extension.

Score: _____

Notes: _____

_____

46. Will the following code snippet successfully compile? Why or why not?

```
Class A {
    static void foo(int x) {};
}
Class B extends A {
    void foo(int x) {};
}
```

Skill Level: Intermediate

Expected answer: No; it is not possible to override a static method with a non-static method. In the above code, the foo() method in class B is attempting to override the foo() method in class A. This is not permitted in Java.

Score: _____

Notes: _____

_____

47. In a JAR file, what is the optional META-INF directory used for?

Skill Level: Intermediate

Expected answer: JAR files are not simply used to archive class and/or resource files. JAR files can contain an optional META-INF directory that contains files and directories in this directory that are recognized and used by the Java 2 platform to configure applications, package and extension configuration, versioning, security, class loaders, and services. The files in this directory can be thought of as building blocks for applications and extensions.

Score: _____

Notes: _____

_____

48. Which package in the Java API can be used to programmatically create a JAR file?

Skill Level: Intermediate

Expected answer: `java.util.jar`

Score: _____

Notes: _____

_____

49. What are the four types of methods in Java that cannot be overridden?

Skill Level: Intermediate

Expected answer:

- private methods
- static methods
- final methods
- methods within final classes

Score: _____

Notes: _____

_____

50. What is the difference between the `==` operator and the `equals()` method?

Skill Level: Intermediate

Expected answer: The `==` operator is used to compare object references. It is not and cannot be used to compare the contents of an object. Keep in mind that the `==` operator also works for comparing primitive data types, but that is not important within the context of this answer.

In the following code, the two Integer objects are not the same when compared using the == operator. Although they have the same content, they are two different object references:

```
Integer i1 = new Integer(42);
Integer i2 = new Integer(42);
if (i1 == i2) // will return false
```

When you want to compare two objects (the contents of the object) for equivalence, you will need to use the equals() method. The equals() method is found in the Object class and is therefore available to all objects. The developer should override the equals() method to include the code that checks whether two objects are equivalent. The default implementation of the equals() method is to compare memory addresses to see if two object are equals. This is usually not what determines if two objects are equal.

Score: _____

Notes: _____

_____

51. What is *Bytecode* and what are its benefits?

Skill Level: Intermediate

Expected answer: *Bytecode* is computer *object code* that is processed by a program called a *virtual machine*. It is important to recognize that bytecode is not machine code used by the hardware processor. The virtual machine will convert bytecode into specific machine instructions that the computer's processor will understand.

In Java, when you compile Java source code using javacc, it is compiled into a .class file that contains bytecode. A Java Virtual Machine (JVM) is then used to read bytecode (contained in the .class binary file) to machine instructions for the platform.

Using languages that come with a virtual machine for each platform has one great benefit. Source code need only to be compiled once and will run on any platform without needing recompiled. This is unlike other computer languages like C and C++ that compile programs directly to machine code. The problem is that you require a separate compiler for each computer platform — that is, for each computer operating system and the hardware set of instructions that it is built on.

Score: _____

Notes: _____

_____

52. Is it possible for a Java program to run out of memory even with the garbage collector active?

Skill Level: Intermediate

Expected answer: Yes. The garbage collector is not a guarantee that you will never run out of memory or ever get a memory leak. One example of a memory leak can occur if an unused (but valid) reference to an unused object is left hanging around in a method that runs for a very long time or in some cases, forever. It is also possible for an application to use up memory resources faster than they can be garbage collected.

Score: _____

Notes: _____

_____

53. Will calling the `System.gc()` method guarantee the garbage collector will collect and remove all unused objects from the memory heap?

Skill Level: Intermediate

Expected answer: No. Calling `System.gc()` only provides a hint to the runtime that now is a good time to run the garbage collector. When control returns from the `System.gc()` method call, the JVM (runtime) has made a best effort to execute the garbage collector at that time and what type of garbage collection to run.

Score: _____

Notes: _____

54. What is the purpose of the `finalize()` method?

Skill Level: Intermediate

Expected answer: Every class inherits the `finalize()` method from `java.lang.Object`. The garbage collector uses this method when it determines that no more references to the object exist. You should override this method to clean-up non-Java resources like closing a file.

Score: _____

Notes: _____

_____

55. If an object is still reachable, can the object's `finalize()` method be invoked by either the garbage collector or other objects?

Skill Level: Intermediate

Expected answer: If the object is still reachable, then the garbage collector cannot invoke its `finalize()` method. However, other object's `finalize()` method can be invoked by other objects.

Score: _____

Notes: _____

_____

56. How many times may the garbage collector call an object's `finalize()` method?

Skill Level: Intermediate

Expected answer: The garbage collector will call an object's `finalize()` method only once.

Score: _____

Notes: _____

_____

57. In a `try-catch-finally` statement, what is the purpose of the `finally` clause?

Skill Level: Intermediate

Expected answer: The `finally` clause is used to provide the capability for your application to execute a piece of code no matter if the try block executed successfully or an exception was thrown or caught.

Score: _____

Notes: _____

_____

58. What is the command-line option with Sun's SDK that can be used to print a message to standard output each time a Java class is loaded?

Skill Level: Intermediate

Expected answer: The option is `-verbose`.

Score: _____

Notes: _____

_____

59. Are classes that are in the same package able to access each other's protected members?

Skill Level: Intermediate

Expected answer: Yes.

Score: _____

Notes: _____

_____

60. What does a *default* member mean?

Skill Level: Intermediate

Expected answer: A *default* member is one that doesn't have any of the following keyword modifiers: `public`, `protected`, or `private`.

61. Which statement in Java causes a program to go back to the statement that began the loop (thereby incrementing the counter) and then to keep going from that point?

Skill Level: Intermediate

Expected answer: The statement is `continue`.

62. What is the difference between the `break` and `continue` statement in Java?

Skill Level: Intermediate

Expected answer: Both statements are used to control the flow of a loop by performing unconditional jumps out of the loop or conditional statement.

The break statement is used to quit the loop without executing any of the remaining statements in the loop; exiting the loop entirely.

The continue statement stops execution of the current iteration and goes back to the beginning of the loop to began the next iteration.

63. What are the range of values returned by the `Math.random()` method?

   Skill Level: Intermediate

   Expected answer: The `Math.random()` method returns a `double` type value in the range of [0,1). The number of values between 0.0 and 1.0 includes the number 0.0, but does not include the number 1.0.

   There are approximately 262 different double fractions that occur between 0 and 1.

64. What is the value returned from the following statement?

   ```
   Math.ceil(Math.PI);
   ```

   Skill Level: Intermediate

   Expected answer: The value is 4.

65. Which access is more restrictive, *default* or *protected*?

   Skill Level: Intermediate

   Expected answer: D*efault* access is more restrictive.

   Score: _____

   Notes: _____

   _____

66. Consider a class named `MyClass` with a final static variable named `b`. It is possible to have four instances of `MyClass`, each of which has a different value for `b`?

   Skill Level: Intermediate

   Expected answer: No, it is not possible.

   Score: _____

   Notes: _____

   _____

67. What is the resulting type when a `byte` is added to a `char` variable?

   Skill Level: Intermediate

   Expected answer: The resulting type is `int`.

   Score: _____

   Notes: _____

   _____

68. If a `char` type is divided by a `long` type, what is the resulting type?

   Skill Level: Intermediate

   Expected answer: The resulting type is `long`.

69. What is a `transient` variable?

Skill Level: Intermediate

Expected answer: By declaring a variable as `transient`, you are indicating to the JVM that this variable is not part of the persistent state of the object and cannot be serialized.

70. Consider an abstract class named `Parent` that contains an abstract method named `methodA()`. If you subclass `Parent`, does your new subclass have to implement `methodA()`?

Skill Level: Intermediate

Expected answer: No. The new subclass does not have to implement `methodA()`, but the new subclass must be declared as `abstract` if it does not implement `methodA()`.

71. Consider any of the signed data types. Are there any equal number of non-zero positive numbers and negative values available?

Skill Level: Intermediate

Expected answer: No.

72. What is the range of values that can be assigned to a `short` variable?

    Skill Level: Intermediate

    Expected answer: The range of values is -2^{15} through $2^{15} - 1$.

73. What is the range of values that can be assigned to a `byte` variable?

    Skill Level: Intermediate

    Expected answer: The range of values is -2^7 through $2^7 - 1$.

74. Consider the following snippet of code:

```
int x, a = 3, b=5;
x = ++a + b++;
```

    After executing both lines, what are the values a, b, and x?

    Skill Level: Intermediate

Expected answer: (Note: Keep in mind that when computing x, a will be incremented by one before assignment, but incrementing b by one will not happen until the assignment is complete.)

```
a=4
b=6
x=9
```

Score: _____

Notes: _____

_____

75. You have determined that several mathematical functions should have been part of the `java.lang.Math` class. You decide to extend the `Math` class to add your new functions. What happens?

Skill Level: Intermediate

Expected answer: Your approach would fail, as it is not possible to extend the `java.lang.Math` class. The `java.lang.Math` class is declared as final and therefore cannot be subclassed.

Score: _____

Notes: _____

_____

76. You want to use several functions in the `java.lang.Math` class. Is it necessary to import `java.lang.Math` in your Java source code? Why or why not?

Skill Level: Intermediate

Expected answer: No, all classes in the `java.lang` package are automatically imported for you.

77. Is it possible to create an instance of the `java.lang.Math` class? Explain why or why not.

    Skill Level: Intermediate

    Expected answer: No, it is not possible to create an instance of the `java.lang.Math` class since its constructor is declared as `private`. Also keep in mind that since all of the methods in the `java.lang.Math` class are static, there is never a need to create an instance of this class in order to use its functions.

    Score: _____

    Notes: _____

    _____

78. Consider a `String` object named `str1` that contains the value of `Retesting`. Write a statement that would return the `String` `test` from `str1`.

    Skill Level: Intermediate

    Expected answer:

    ```
    String str2 = str1.substring(2,6);
    ```

    Score: _____

    Notes: _____

    _____

79. Are overloaded methods allowed to change the access level?

Skill Level: High

Expected answer: Yes.

Score: _____

Notes: _____

_____

80. Is the following a valid statement? Why or why not?

```
int x = 1; x = !x;
```

Skill Level: High

Expected answer: No, the use of the ! operator is not appropriate since x is an int type, not a Boolean.

Score: _____

Notes: _____

_____

81. Is the third line in the following code snippet legal? If so, what is the value of x, and describe what happens when assigning x.

```
String x = "Testing";
int y = 5;
x += y;
```

Skill Level: High

Expected answer: Yes, it is legal Java. The value x will be assigned the String **Testing5**.

The third line will attempt to add an int to a String, which will result in a conversion of the int (in this case, 5) to a String. Then a concatenation of two String objects occurs.

---

82. What is the value of x in the following code snippet?

```
int x = 19 % 5;
```

Skill Level: High

Expected answer: The value of x is 4. Dividing 19 by 5 gives remainder 4, this being the result of the modulo expression.

83. What is the value returned by the statement `Math.ceil(-17.8)`?

Skill Level: High

Expected answer: `-17.0`. (Note: This question has a "High" skill level since it requires the candidate to know that the return value is a `double`. The answer is returned as a `double` (`-17.0`) and not as the `int` value `17`.)

84. What is the value returned by the statement `Math.floor(13.2)`?

Skill Level: High

Expected answer: `-13.0`. (Note: This question has a "High" skill level since it requires the candidate to know that the return value is a `double`. The answer is returned as a `double` (`-13.0`) and not as the `int` value `13`.)

Score: _____

Notes: _____

_____

85. Consider the following code snippet:

```
String      name1 = "Alex";
StringBuffer name2 = new StringBuffer("Alex");
```

How would you compare the contents of name1 and name2 to determine if they are equal?

Skill Level: High

Expected answer:

```
Boolean b = name1.equals(name2.toString());
```

Unlike the String class, StringBuffer does not override the equals() method. If you did not convert name2 to a String first, you would only implement this string by comparing object references.

Score: _____

Notes: _____

_____

86. Consider the class declaration:

```
Class Student extends Person
```

What is the order in which each of the constructors is invoked, including the Object class?

Skill Level: High

Expected answer: `Student` constructor is invoked, followed by the `Person` constructor, followed by the `Object` constructor.

Constructors are always invoked beginning with the object being created (in this case, `Student`), followed by chained invocations, to superclass constructors moving up the inheritance tree, and always ending with the Object class.

Score: _____

Notes: _____

_____

87. What is the value returned by the statement `Math.round(14.34)`?

Skill Level: High

Expected answer: `14`. (Note: This question has a "High" skill level since it requires the candidate to know that the return value is an `integer`. The answer is returned as an `integer` (`14`) and not as a `double` value `14.0`.)

Score: _____

Notes: _____

_____

88. Will the following class compile? If not, how would you fix it to compile?

```
abstract class Parent  {
public abstract void methodA() {};
}
```

Skill Level: High

Expected answer: This class will not compile. The Java compiler will complain that the abstract method methodA() cannot contain any body.

To fix the code, you could simply remove the two braces from methodA().

Score: _____

Notes: _____

_____

89. When creating an abstract class, must the class contain at least one abstract method before it will compile?

Skill Level: High

Expected answer: No.

Score: _____

Notes: _____

_____

90. If you have a class that contains one or more final methods, must the class be declared final? Explain why or why not.

Skill Level: High

Expected answer: No, it is not a requirement to declare a class as final if it has any final methods. You would declare a class final only if you did not want the class to be subclassed. By declaring a method as final, you are saying that its implementation is constant, meaning that the method cannot be overridden.

Score: _____

Notes: _____

_____

91. The signature of the `sin()` method of the `Math` class is as follows:

```
public static double sin(double angle)
```

What unit of measure is the angle argument?

Skill Level: High

Expected answer: The unit of measure is `Radians`.

Score: _____

Notes: _____

_____

92. Will the following produce a compile-time error? If so, how would you fix it?

```
float pi = 3.142;
```

Skill Level: High

Expected answer: Yes. Since the value 3.142 is treated as `double`, you must explicitly cast to `float`.

```
float pi = (float) 3.142;
```

Score: _____

Notes: _____

_____

Java Installation and Configuration

1. What is the Web address (URL) where you can download Sun's official Java Software Development Kit (SDK) J2SE?

    Skill Level: Low

    Expected answer:

    > The URL is http://java.sun.com.

    Score: _____

    Notes: _____

    _____

2. Using Sun's Java 2 SDK, how do you check which version of the SDK you are using?

    Skill Level: Low

    Expected answer: You can check the version by using `java - version`.

    Score: _____

    Notes: _____

    _____

3. After installing the Java 2 SDK bundle, what are the most important environment variables that should be set?

    Skill Level: Low

    Expected answer:

    - `JAVA_HOME` — Points to the directory where you installed the Java SDK For example, `JAVA_HOME=c:\j2sdk1.4.1_01`

    - `PATH` — Should contain the bin directory of your Java SDK. For example, `PATH=%PATH%;%JAVA_HOME%/bin`

- **CLASSPATH** – Should contain the directories and Java archives where the JVM will look for Java class files to load.

Score: _____

Notes: _____

_____

4. What is the environment variable CLASSPATH used for?

Skill Level: Intermediate

Expected answer: This is an environment variable that can be set to contain the directories and archive used by the Java interpreter and the Java compiler when searching for packages and classes on the local machine.

Keep in mind that the CLASSPATH environment variable can contain directories and/or java class archive files (JAR and ZIP files).

Score: _____

Notes: _____

_____

5. If you do not set CLASSPATH, what value will be used by the JVM to locate and load Java class files by default?

Skill Level: Intermediate

Expected answer: Only the current directory, "." is included. Ensure that if you do set the CLASSPATH path, you will need to explicitly include the current directory (".") if you want it in the CLASSPATH.

Score: _____

Notes: _____

_____

6. If the CLASSPATH environment variable is set and the -classpath option is used for the JRE, which one takes precedence?

   Skill Level: Intermediate

   Expected answer: The -classpath option takes precedence over the CLASSPATH environment variable.

   Score: _____

   Notes: _____

   _____

Java Performance Tuning

1. Sun's JDK includes a minimal profiler. What command-line option is used with the Java executable to invoke this profiler with Sun's JDK 1.2 or later version?

   Skill Level: Low

   Expected answer: Using Sun's JDK 1.2 or later, use the `Java` executable with the `-Xrunhprof` option. (Using versions of the JDK earlier than 1.2, the command-line option is `-prof`.)

   Score: _____

   Notes: _____

   _____

2. A common mistake programmers make is to perform "premature optimization" – trying to optimize code during code development. Why is this a bad idea?

   Skill Level: Low

   Expected answer: The rule here is to simply develop code to work — make it correct and get it finished. Optimization is something that should be performed after development and only if there are known bottlenecks. It is easy to use tools to measure for bottlenecks. During development, it is hard to know where the bottlenecks will exist, if at all, in your code. Many developers and programmers waste unnecessary time during development trying to optimize code that will not be perceived by the end user. In many cases, the code that you develop will be fast enough.

   Score: _____

   Notes: _____

   _____

3. What methods can you call in Java to encourage or suggest to the *garbage collector* that it reclaim memory?

Skill Level: Low

Expected answer: There are two methods that can send a request to the garbage collector asking it to reclaim memory: `java.lang.System.gc()` or `java.lang.Runtime.getRuntime().gc()`. The accepted convention is to invoke `System.gc()`, which is equivalent to `Runtime.getRuntime().gc()`.

Score: _____

Notes: _____

_____

4. What is the command-line option with Sun's SDK that can be used to print out messages by the interpreter each time a garbage collection is performed?

Skill Level: Intermediate

Expected answer: The option is `-verbosegc`.

Score: _____

Notes: _____

_____

5. When tuning an application, you should monitor and determine if the application is limiting any of the three major computer resources. What are these three computer resources?

Skill Level: Intermediate

Expected answer:

- CPU availability

- System (RAM) memory

- I/O (Disk, network, etc)

Score: _____

Notes: _____

_____

6. When using the default profiler packaged with Sun's JDK 1.2 (or later), what is the default name of the results file that contains the profile data?

   Skill Level: Intermediate

   Expected answer: With Sun's JDK 1.2 or later, the default file name is `java.hprof.txt`. (If versions of the JDK earlier than 1.2 are used, the default file name is `java.prof`.)

   Score: _____

   Notes: _____

   _____

7. When using the default profiler packaged with Sun's JDK 1.2 (or later), is it possible to specify the name of the results file that will contain the profile data? If so, what does the command-line option look like?

   Skill Level: Intermediate

   Expected answer: Yes, it is possible. The option would look like `-Xrunhprof:file=filename`. (Using versions of the JDK earlier than 1.2, the option would like `-prof:filename`.)

   Score: _____

   Notes: _____

   _____

8. What is a Just-In-Time compiler and what are the benefits to using it?

Skill Level: Intermediate

Expected answer: When using the JVM, the bytecode must be processed and interpreted one instruction at a time. A Just-In-Time (JIT) compiler can take Java bytecode and recompile it for a particular system platform. Using JIT will often enable the Java program to run faster.

Score: _____

Notes: _____

_____

9. What is the difference between the StringBuffer class and the String class?

Skill Level: Intermediate

Expected answer: Both classes support the use of storing and manipulating strings — character data consisting of more than one character. Both classes contain similar methods for manipulating strings and converting them to other variables.

A String object is immutable, which means you cannot change it. In a Java program, you may update a String object, but this will cause excessive computing cycles since behind the scenes, Java is creating a new String object to hold the new value. String concatenation via the +operator is one of the most convenient things to do in Java, but as you can see, is also one of the most expensive in terms of memory and performance.

The StringBuffer class provides for strings that can be modified. The StringBuffer class will grow and shrink to match the size of the file. You should use String buffers when you know that the value of the character data will change. This can occur in an application when you are constructing character data dynamically. Take for example, reading text data from a file or values from a database query.

Score: _____

Notes: _____

_____

10. What method in the `StringBuffer` class can be used to append character data to the end of the current data already within the `StringBuffer` object?

   Skill Level: Low

   Expected answer: The `append(String str)` method can be used.

   Score: _____

   Notes: _____

   _____

11. How would you return the content of a `StringBuffer` object into a `String` object?

   Skill Level: Low

   Expected answer: *Expected answer:* Use the toString() method of StringBuffer to return its contents to a String object.

   Score: _____

   Notes: _____

   _____

12. Consider the following code snippet:

```
int x = 8;
int y = x/4;
```

Using bit-wise arithmetic, could you replace the operation in the second line with a faster and more efficient operation without changing the meaning of the statement?

Skill Level: High

Expected answer: *Expected answer:*   Simply perform two right shifts of the x value:

int y = x >> 2;

Each right shift by one is equivalent to dividing by 2. In our example, $2^2 = 4$; so perform two right shifts.

Score: _____

Notes: _____

_____

13. Consider the following code snippet:

```
int x = 4;
int y - x ^ 8;
```

Using bit-wise arithmetic, could you replace the operation in the second line with a faster and more efficient operation without changing the meaning of the statement?

Skill Level: High

Expected answer: Yes, simply perform three left shifts of the x value:

```
int y = x << 3;
```

Each left shift by one is equivalent to multiplying by 2. In this example, $2^3 = 8$, so you should perform 3 left shifts.

Score: _____

Notes: _____

_____

14. Consider the following code snippet:

```
for (int i = 0; i < j.length; i++) {
j[i] = k * Math.sqrt(z);
}
```

Can you see any improvements that can be made to increase the efficiency of this code?

Skill Level: High

Expected answer: As you can see in the previous loop, the elements of the array are being assigned the same value with each iteration. Not only is it the same value each time, it is being calculated each time, producing the same results. Since the calculation produces the same value each time, you should simply move the calculation out of the loop, calculating it only once. Then, you should assign it to a variable and use the variable in the loop as follows:

```
double z1 = k * Math.sqrt(z);
for (int i = 0; i < j.length; i++) {
j[i] = z1;
}
```

Score: _____

Notes: _____

_____

Java Security

1. Many books and articles that discuss Java security use the term, *Java Sandbox*. What is meant by this term?

   Skill Level: Low

   Expected answer: The term, Java Sandbox is often used to describe the security model used by Java when running programs. The idea behind this model is to provide an interface between a Java application and operating system resources (file system, network, memory, and so on) that can be configured by a system administrator or end user.

   When you allow a Java program to be run on your computer, you want it to run within an environment in which you control to what it has access. This environment (or *sandbox*) can be configured by an end user or system administrator to constrain the operating resources to which the Java program has access. The Java program is therefore confined to work within a *sandbox* that is responsible for protecting those system resources as defined by the constraints imposed upon it from the end user and system administrator.

   Score: _____

   Notes: _____

   _____

2. Prior to Java 2, what was the only type of Java application that could run in a *sandbox* environment used to protect system resources?

   Skill Level: Low

   Expected answer: Prior to Java 2, the only type of applications that could run within a security model (or sandbox) were Java applets that ran within a Java enabled browser. The purpose of this was to protect operating system resources (file systems, network connections, and soon) from downloaded applets. With Java 2, all programs (e.g., Java standalone applications, command-line application, applets) have the option of running within a security model (or sandbox).

Score: _____

Notes: _____

_____

3. If no security options are set when starting the application what is the default security manager used by the JVM?

Skill Level: Low

Expected answer: The default is None. If no security options are set when starting an application, there is no security manager for it. When starting an application and no security manager is installed, no restrictions are placed on any activities requested of the Java API; the Java API will do whatever it is asked.

Score: _____

Notes: _____

_____

4. When starting a Java application, how many security managers can be installed for it?

Skill Level: Low

Expected answer: Only one security manager can be installed for a given Java application. A single security manager, however, can establish multiple security policies.

Score: _____

Notes: _____

_____

5. What is the name of the command-line property and at what value should it be set to install the default (built-in) security manager when starting a Java application?

Skill Level: Low

Expected answer: When starting a Java application, you can define the property `java.security.manager` to specify which security manager to use for the application. If you want to install the default (built-in) security manager, simply define the property with no value as shown below. There are several other ways the `java.security.manager` property can be set to install the default security manager, which are also shown as follows:

```
java -Djava.security.manager  myApp
java -Djava.security.manager=""  myApp
java -Djava.security.manager=default  myApp
```

Score: _____

Notes: _____

_____

6. What is the difference between the `SecurityManager` and `AccessController` elements of Java's security model?

Skill Level: Intermediate

Expected answer: Both elements exist in Java's security model to allow (or prevent) most of the access from Java's core API to a computer's operating systems resources based on policies defined by the end user and/or system administrator. The `SecurityManager` class allows applications to implement a security policy. The `SecurityManager` interface exists mostly for historical purposes and is being replaced by the `AccessController` class. Most of the actions of the `SecurityManager` are deferred to the `AccessController`.

For now, all of the check methods in `SecurityManager` are still supported; however, most of their definitions have been changed to call the new `SecurityManager` `checkPermission()` method, whose default implementation calls the `AccessController` `checkPermission()` method. It should be noted that certain internal security checks may stay in the `SecurityManager` class, unless until they can be parameterized correctly

The `SecurityManager` interface will continue to be backwards compatible with Java applications that may have written their own `SecurityManager` classes based on earlier versions of the JDK. Although `SecurityManager` remains backwards compatible, it is strongly recommended that `AccessController` be used for security policy enforcement as it provides for a more flexible mechanism with its use of security policy files. It is also much easier to implement fine-grained permissions on specific classes. Use `SecurityManager` as a last resort.

Score: _____

Notes: _____

_____

7. What package would you find the `SecurityManager` class defined in?

Skill Level: Low

Expected answer: The package is `java.lang`.

Score: _____

Notes: _____

_____

8. When one of the check methods in the `SecurityManager` determines that the operation it is checking is not permitted, what exception is thrown?

   Skill Level: Low

   Expected answer: The exception thrown is `SecurityException`.

   Score: _____

   Notes: _____

   _____

9. When one of the check methods in the `SecurityManager` determines that the operation it is checking is not permitted, it throws the exception `SecurityException`. What is the one check method that is an exception to this convention?

   Skill Level: High

   Expected answer: The `checkTopLevelWindow()` method does not throw a `SecurityException`. This method returns `False` if the `calling` Thread is not trusted to bring up the top-level window indicated by the window argument. Otherwise, this method returns `True`.

   Score: _____

   Notes: _____

   _____

10. Do you have to wrap the check methods that throw a `SecurityException` exception of `SecurityManager` in a try-catch block? Why or why not?

Skill Level: Intermediate

Expected answer: The `SecurityManager` class subclasses `RuntimeException`. Keep in mind that `Runtime` exceptions are different from others in that they do not have to be caught.

Score: _____

Notes: _____

_____

11. What two methods available in the `System` class allow you to retrieve and install a Security Manager?

Skill Level: Intermediate

Expected answer:

```
public static SecurityManager getSecurityManager()
```

This method is used to return a reference to the currently installed `SecurityManager` object.

```
public static void setSecurityManager(
SecurityManager sm)
```

This method is used to set the system's `SecurityManager` to the object passed.

Score: _____

Notes: _____

_____

12. If you are running an application with no `SecurityManager` installed and call the `System.getSecurityManager()` method, what is returned?

Skill Level: Intermediate

Expected answer: What is returned is `null`.

Score: _____

Notes: _____

_____

13. Before attempting to install a `SecurityManager` using the `System.setSecurityManager()` method, what runtime permission must you have in order to instantiate the `SecurityManager` object?

Skill Level: High

Expected answer: The permission is `createSecurityManager`.

Score: _____

Notes: _____

_____

14. What method from the `SystemManager` class is used to check if the calling Thread is allowed to write to the specified file descriptor?

Skill Level: High

Expected answer:

The method used is `void checkWrite(FileDescriptor fd.)`

Score: _____

Notes: _____

_____

15. What is the name of the property that could be set on the command-line to specify the policy files to be utilized when starting an application?

Skill Level: Low

Expected answer: The property is `java.security.policy`.

For example,

```
java
-Djava.security.policy=/01/app/oracle/java.policy
MyApp
```

Score: _____

Notes: _____

_____

16. When using the `java.security.policy` property, what is the difference between using the equals sign '=' and the double equals sign '==' when specifying the policy file name?

Skill Level: Intermediate

Expected answer: When using the equals sign '=' to specify policy files, you are essentially creating a "final policy" by doing a union of all granted permissions in all policy files. (Remember, this would include the policy files defined in the `java.security` file.)

When using the double equals sign '==' to specify policy files, you are saying to ignore any policy file definitions in the `java.security` file and only use the policy files specified. The following example will only use the policy `myJava.policy` file when creating the "final policy":

```
-Djava.security.policy==myJava.policy
```

17. What is the default name of the policy file?

   Skill Level: Low

   Expected answer: `java.policy`

18. What is the name of the GUI tool included with Sun's JDK that allows a user to create policy files?

   Skill Level: Low

   Expected answer: The GUI tool is `policytool`.

19. What is the name and location of the global policy file that will be applied to all applications run by any system user?

   Skill Level: Low

   Expected answer: The name and location are `${JAVA_HOME}/jre/lib/security/java.policy`.

20. What is the name of the property that could be set to print trace messages by the Java 2 security system during runtime? What would be the main reason for setting this property?

Skill Level: Low

Expected answer: The property is `java.security.debug`.

Setting the `java.security.debug` property is useful to capture a trace of messages from the Java 2 system security layer. Most developers use this option when a security exception is thrown or a signed application is not working and they need to troubleshoot and debug the program.

Score: _____

Notes: _____

_____

21. What is the file `java.security` used for and where is it typically located?

Skill Level: Low

Expected answer: The `java.security` file is typically located in `$JAVA_HOME/jre/lib/security`. This file is used as the "master security properties file" to store all security properties used by Java's security model.

Here is a list of some of the properties that can be set:

- The name and location of the default system-wide policy files (policy.url.1, policy.url.2,…)

- Default login configuration file (login.config.url.1)

- Whether or not to allow an extra policy to be passed on the command line (policy.allowSystemProperty=true/false)

Score: _____

Notes: _____

_____

22. What is the bytecode verifier and why is it important within the context of Java security?

Skill Level*:* Intermediate

Expected answer*:* The bytecode verifier is invoked at execution time (after the class loader). It is one of the links (specifically the second link) in a chain of layers used in enforcing the rules of the Java language. It is important to understand that the bytecode verifier does not completely guarantee that the bytecode will follow all of the rules of the Java language. Some of the tests to ensure that rules are being followed are deferred to the JVM.

The bytecode verifier is extremely useful when dealing with Java application security. . While the compiler does a pretty good job of enforcing the rules of the Java language, it can't do everything. First, it cannot enforce array bounds checking, nor can it validate all cases of illegal castings. Both of these can be huge security holes used to exploit the security of your computer. Consider a compiled Java application you are about to run that came from an unknown source. Can you be certain that the class files bytecode is legal and does not exploit a security hole by ignoring certain rules in the Java language that was meant to be protected? Someone who wants to exploit security holes in your system could write an *evil* (sometimes referred to as a *hostile*) compiler to produce illegal Java bytecode that would bypass certain constraints on the Java language and expose your system. This is where the bytecode verifier comes into play. By default, the Java Runtime environment does not trust the incoming bytecode and will run it through the bytecode verifier to ensure the bytecode follows the Java language.

Score: _____

Notes: _____

_____

23. What are some of the items that the bytecode verifier is responsible for checking and proving?

Skill Level: Intermediate

Expected answer: The bytecode verifier is responsible for ensuring the incoming bytecode about to be executed conforms to legal Java instructions. Here is a list of some of the items the bytecode verifier is responsible for proving:

- Ensure that the bytecode has the correct format as defined in the JVM specification. For example, does the class file have the correct length, magic numbers in the correct places, and so on.

- Ensure that every class has a single superclass (except for `java.lang.Object`).

- Ensure there are no illegal primitive data conversions (i.e., trying to convert a `float` to `Object`).

- Ensure there are no illegal data conversion of objects (i.e., all casts are being performed legally).

- Ensure all final classes are not subclasses.

- Ensure all final methods are not overridden.

- Ensure that the operand stack does not overflow or underflow.

24. The JVM maintains two stacks for each Thread of execution. What are these two stacks and which is the only one that can be validated to not underflow or overflow by the bytecode verifier?

Skill Level: High

Expected answer: The JVM maintains two stacks for each Thread:

- The data stack. This stack holds a series of method frames, and each method frame holds its local variables and other storage for its method invocation.

- The operand stack. This stack holds the values on which the Java bytecode operates. Each method invocation requires this stack and itself is allocated on the data stack.

The only one of these stacks that the bytecode verifier can guarantee will never overflow or underflow is the operand stack. The bytecode verifier cannot protect against overflow of the data stack, especially in the case of an infinitely recursive method.

25. What is a *message digest*, and for what are they primarily used?

Skill Level: High

Expected answer: A message digest (sometimes called a digital fingerprint, a hash, or simply a digest) is a small sequence of bytes that produced when a given set of data (called the message) is passed through a message digest engine. A message digest engine takes data as an ordered set of bytes and produces a single output called the message digest. It is often said that the message digest represents the data that was used to create it. The message digest is of little use without the original data (the message) that was used to create it.

If even one byte of the original message is changed and run through the message digest engine again, the message digest will be completely different from the message digest that was created with the original message. Typically, a message digest engine is used to verify that a particular message has not changed. For example, to ensure that a document has not been changed, run the questionable document through the message digest engine again, and compare its output (the message digest) with the original message that the author created from the original document.

Score: _____

Notes: _____

_____

26. What are some of the more common message digest algorithms?

Skill Level: High

Expected answer:

- MD5
- SHA
- SHA1
- SHA-1

Score: _____

Notes: _____

_____

27. Write a method called performRot13() that implements the rot13 algorithm. Here is the signature of the method to implement:

```
String performRot13(String in);
```

Skill Level: High

Expected answer:

```
public static String doConvert(String in) {
StringBuffer tempReturn = new StringBuffer();
int abyte = 0;

for (int i=0; i<in.length(); i++) {
abyte = in.charAt(i);
int cap = abyte & 32;
abyte &= ~cap;
abyte = ( (abyte >= 'A')
&&
abyte <= 'Z')
?
((abyte - 'A' + 13) % 26 + 'A')
:
abyte) | cap;
tempReturn.append((char)abyte);
}
return tempReturn.toString();
}
```

Score: _____

Notes: _____

_____

28. Which package contains classes and interfaces for parsing and managing certificates, certificate revocation lists (CRLs), and certification paths?

Skill Level: Low

Expected answer: The package is `java.security.cert`

Score: _____

Notes: _____

_____

29. Which package contains the interfaces for generating DSA and RSA keys?

Skill Level: High

Expected answer: The package is `java.security.interfaces`.

Score: _____

Notes: _____

_____

Java Threads

1. What is a *Thread*?

    Skill Level: Low

    Expected answer: The term Thread is shorthand for Thread of control, and is defined as a section of code executed independently of other Threads of control, all within a single program (or process). Other terms used to signify a Thread are execution context or lightweight process. You can also think of a Thread as the path taken by a program during execution.

    Multiple Threads of control can execute within a program. Think about a program that has to execute tasks from two different lists. In a multithreaded application, both lists will be executed within two different Threads. Both Threads will be processed in their correct order. However, the scheduler will work on one task for a while and then switch to the second Thread, intending to return to the point at which it left off in the first Thread at some future time.

    Score: _____

    Notes: _____

    _____

2. What does the phrase *Thread safe* mean and why is it so important in Java?

    Skill Level: Low

    Expected answer: This phrase is used to describe a method that can run safely in a multithreaded environment without unwanted interaction between the Threads.

Thread safety is of particular importance to Java programmers, since Java is a programming language that provides built-in support for Threads. Developers should take care when programming with multiple Threads to ensure routines are Thread safe. They should ensure that the risk that one Thread will interfere and modify data of another Thread is removed. Also, they should use methods that coordinate access to shared data to eliminate potential race conditions.

Score: _____

Notes: _____

_____

3. What is the difference between *green Threads* and *native Threads*?

Skill Level: Low

Expected answer: Green Threads are a technique in which the Thread mechanism is implemented within the JVM itself. The JVM is unaware of any Thread support of the operating system and is meant to support Threading on any OS. Using this technique, all green Threads are run in one native Thread, and all scheduling is implemented by the JVM. The major disadvantage to green Threads is for SMP systems, in which the Java application is limited to only one processor.

Native Threads, on the other hand, is a mechanism that provides Threading support using the OS Threading implementation. This allows the Java application to use features of hardware and the OS, and therefore improves performance.

Score: _____

Notes: _____

_____

4. Which package contains the `Thread` class?

   Skill Level: Low

   Expected answer: The `java.lang` package contains the `Thread` class.

   Score: _____

   Notes: _____

   _____

5. What are the two basic approaches for writing code that creates a new Thread of control?

   Skill Level: Low

   Expected answer:

   - Extend the `Thread` `class defined` in the `java.lang` package and override the `run()` method.

   - Implement the `Runnable` interface provided in the `java.lang` package, and therefore implement the `run()` method. (In this case, the `Runnable` object provides the `run()` method to the Thread.)

   Score: _____

   Notes: _____

   _____

6. If you have a class that must subclass another class (i.e., applet), which strategy must you use to create another Thread?

Skill Level: Low

Expected answer: Since multiple inheritance is not available in Java, you must implement the `Runnable` interface.

Score: _____

Notes: _____

_____

7. After extending the `Thread` class to create a new Thread, what method must you override in the `Thread` class to define the code to be executed by the new Thread?

Skill Level: Low

Expected answer: You will need to override the `run()` method of the `Thread` class with the code that will run in the newly created Thread.

Score: _____

Notes: _____

_____

8. What is the signature of the `run()` method in the `Thread` class?

Skill Level: Low

Expected answer: The signature is `public void run()`.

Score: _____

Notes: _____

_____

9. Which interface does the Thread class implement?

Skill Level: Low

Expected answer: The Thread class implements the `Runnable` interface.

Score: _____

Notes: _____

_____

10. Within your program, you've just created a Thread object named myThread. What method would you use to call on this object to start it as a separate Thread of execution?

Skill Level: Low

Expected answer: You would use `myThread.start();`.

Score: _____

Notes: _____

_____

11. What key method in a Thread is called by the `start()` method?

Skill Level: Low

Expected answer: The method is `run();`.

Score: _____

Notes: _____

_____

12. For what purpose are Thread groups used?

Skill Level: Low

Expected answer: Thread groups provide the developer with an effective method of collecting multiple Threads into a single object. This enables the developer to manage multiple Threads simultaneously, rather than managing them separately. All Threads in Java are a member of a Thread group. For example, you can set maximum priority levels, call `suspend()`, and `interrupt()` on Threads in a group. You can also give a good name to a Thread group to help you easily track and debug your programs.

If your Java application creates many Threads that should be manipulated as a group, or if you are implementing a custom security manager, you will likely want more control over these Threads using Thread groups.

Originally, Thread groups were created for security reasons. It was assumed that code from third-party companies could not be trusted and would run in a dedicated Thread group. Your code would thus be protected by not allowing Threads from external companies to start, stop, and suspend your Threads. This model was changed in Java, and there is no such protection now.

Score: _____

Notes: _____

_____

Conducting the Java Job Interview

13. For what purpose is the keyword synchronized used?

Skill Level: Low

Expected answer: The keyword `synchronized` provides a solution to protecting object data from being accessed/modified from two different Threads that could possibly leave the object in an invalid state. When a Thread has gained access into a synchronized block of code, it is the only Thread that can exist in this part of the code. The Thread keeps all locks on objects until it either exits the synchronized code or calls the `wait()` method.

When writing a multithread application, you should try to avoid the possibility that a Thread that might be halted in mid-calculation while another Thread attempts to use that data in its inconsistent state.

The synchronized keyword is used to indicate that a method or anonymous block of code should be guarded by the monitor mechanism of the JVM.

Score: _____

Notes: _____

_____

14. What are the high-level states in which a Thread can reside?

Skill Level: Low

Expected answer: The states are ready, running, waiting, and dead.

Score: _____

Notes: _____

_____

15. Say you have a method in a class that is synchronized, and a subclass that is extending this class contains a method that is overriding the synchronized method. Is it mandatory that the new overriding method be declared as synchronized?

Skill Level: Intermediate

Expected answer: No, the method in the subclass that is overriding the synchronized method does not have to be declared as synchronized. The synchronized keyword only affects the code block in the original class.

Score: _____

Notes: _____

_____

16. What is the difference between a *daemon Thread* and a *user Thread?*

Skill Level: Intermediate

Expected answer: The key difference is in how a Java program can be stopped. In most cases, *daemon Threads* are created by the JVM to perform some sort of kind of housekeeping duties (one of the best examples of the daemon Thread is the garbage collector). However, when a Java program contains no more live *user Threads* — no matter how many *daemon Threads* are alive and running in the program — the program will end.

Score: _____

Notes: _____

_____

17. How do you create a daemon Thread?

Skill Level: Intermediate

Expected answer: A daemon Thread is created in much the same way a user Thread is created, except that one property setting is made using the `setDaemon(true)` method. This method must be called after creating the `Thread` object and before it is started, as shown below:

```
Thread myThread = new Thread(this);
myThread.setDaemon(true);
myThread.start();
```

Score: _____

Notes: _____

_____

18. You've just created and started a Thread object named myThread. What method would you call to determine if this Thread is a daemon Thread?

Skill Level: Intermediate

Expected answer:

```
The method is Boolean dt = myThread.isDaemon();.
```

Score: _____

Notes: _____

_____

19. What has happened to the `stop()`, `suspend()`, and `()` methods in Java SDK 1.2?

Skill Level: Intermediate

Expected answer: All three methods have been deprecated as of the Java 2, version 1.2 release.

20. Consider an object named object1 that has several Threads waiting on it. One of the Threads waiting is called thread1. What statement could you use to notify only thread1 without notifying another of the other Threads waiting for object1?

Skill Level: Intermediate

Expected answer: This is not possible. When an object (in this example, `object1`) has multiple Threads waiting for it, there is no way to control which of the waiting Threads will be notified.

Score: _____

Notes: _____

_____

21. What does the `Thread.isAlive()` method tell you about a particular Thread?

Skill Level: Intermediate

Expected answer: The `Thread.isAlive()` method returns a Boolean value indicating whether or not a Thread is alive. The method returns true if this Thread is alive; false if otherwise. A Thread is alive if it has been started and has not yet died. This method often confuses developers. The actual test is to verify if the Thread "was" alive at the moment when you tested it. Many programmers make the mistake of interrupting the `Thread.isAlive()` method as a test to determine whether the Thread "is" alive (running) when invoking the method. This is not the case. To erase the confusion surrounding this method, Sun should rename it, `Thread.wasAlive()`.

Score: _____

Notes: _____

_____

22. If you create a new Thread without specifying its group in the constructor, into what Thread group is it created?

Skill Level: Intermediate

Expected answer: The Java runtime system (JVM) automatically places the new Thread in the same group as the Thread that created it (known as the *current Thread group* and the *current Thread*, respectively). When a Java application first starts, the Java runtime system creates a `ThreadGroup` named `main`. Unless specified otherwise, all new Threads that you create become members of the `main` Thread group.

Score: _____

Notes: _____

_____

23. What method from the Thread class allows you to retrieve the number of active Threads in the current Thread's Thread group?

Skill Level: Intermediate

Expected answer: The `activeCount()` method can be used to return an integer type indicating the number of active Threads in the current Thread's Thread group.

24. Within your main application Thread, you start another Thread that is going to perform a long calculation. After the calculation Thread starts, you continue to perform some secondary tasks within the main Thread. Once your secondary tasks are completed, you must wait for the results of your calculation Thread before you can continue. To perform the wait within the main Thread, you create a loop that contains a combination of the `sleep()` and `isAlive()` methods to poll the calculation Thread to wait for it to complete. Is there a better technique that performs the same method of waiting but in a single API method?

Skill Level*:* Intermediate

Expected answer*:* The `join()` method basically accomplishes the same task as that of combining the `sleep()` and `isAlive()` methods. When using the `join()` technique, we accomplish the same task with a single method call. We also have better control over the timeout interval, and we don't have to waste CPU cycles by polling.

25. Explain how the `join()` method works and give an example of what it's used to accomplish.

Skill Level: Intermediate

Expected answer: The `join()` method provides an efficient way for one Thread to wait for another Thread to complete before it is allowed to continue processing.

Take, for example, starting a Thread to do a long calculation. While this calculation is being made, we are free to do other tasks. Assume that sometime later, we have completed all other secondary tasks and need to deal with the results of the long calculation — we need to wait until the calculation(s) is finished before continuing on to process the results. This is where the join() can help.

When the join() method is called, the current Thread will simply wait until the Thread with which it is joining is no longer alive. (In this case, alive means that the Thread has not been started or stopped by another Thread or the Thread has completed.)

Score: _____

Notes: _____

_____

26. There exists a version of the `join()` operation that uses a single long parameter to specify how long it waits to join another completed Thread before it times out and simply continues. What unit of time does the long parameter use to measure this wait before the `join()` method times out?

Skill Level: Intermediate

Expected answer: The `long` argument is measured in milliseconds.

There is another version of the `join()` method that takes two arguments — a `long` and an `int`. The long is measured in milliseconds and the `int` is measured in nanoseconds. This timeout value is subject to rounding based on the capabilities of the underlying platform.

Score: _____

Notes: _____

_____

27. In what class would you find the methods `sleep()` and `yield()`?

Skill Level: Intermediate

Expected answer: They are found in the `Thread` class.

Score: _____

Notes: _____

_____

28. In what class would you find the methods `notify()`, `notifyAll(,)` and `wait()`?

Skill Level: Intermediate

Expected answer: They are found in the `Object` class.

Score: _____

Notes: _____

_____

29. What is a semaphore?

Skill Level: Intermediate

Expected answer: Any object that can be used by two Threads to communicate with one another in order to synchronize their operations. You can think of a semaphore as a way to send messages using signaling flags.

Score: _____

Notes: _____

_____

30. What will happen if you attempt to call the wait() method on an object on which the Thread does not own the lock?

Skill Level: Intermediate

Expected answer:

The exception `java.lang.IllegalMonitorStateException` will be thrown. A Thread must own the lock on the object before it can call the `wait()` method on that object.

Score: _____

Notes: _____

_____

31. What is meant by the phrase, "race condition"?

Skill Level: Intermediate

Expected answer: A *race condition* occurs when two Threads simultaneously contend for the same object and, as a consequence, leave the object in an undefined or corrupted state depending on which gets to the object first. This happens any time that a sequence of operations must be atomic (not preempt able). Race conditions can be solved by making operations atomic using the `synchronized` keyword.

32. Is it possible to declare a static method to be synchronized?

Skill Level: Intermediate

Expected answer: Yes, a static method can be synchronized. For a Thread to call a static method, it must acquire a lock on the class that owns the method.

33. At any moment, for how many object locks can a Thread be waiting?

Skill Level: Intermediate

Expected answer: Not more than one.

34. If two Threads with different priorities are ready to run, which Thread will be run first? Explain your answer.

Skill Level: Intermediate

Expected answer: It is not possible to tell for certain exactly which Thread will run. At any given moment, the Thread with the highest priority should be running. However, this is not a guarantee. It is possible that the scheduler will choose to run a lower priority Thread to avoid starvation. It is important to use priority only to affect or suggest priority to the scheduling policy for efficiency purpose. As a programmer, you should never rely on Thread priority for algorithm correctness.

Score: _____

Notes: _____

_____

35. Which method can a Thread call to give up its right to execute thereby halting its execution?

Skill Level: Intermediate

Expected answer: The Thread can call the `yield()` method.

Score: _____

Notes: _____

_____

36. Say a Thread attempts to yield the CPU to other Threads, all of which have a lower priority. What happens when Java executes the `yield()` method?

Skill Level: Intermediate

Expected answer: The `yield()` statement is ignored. Threads can only yield the CPU to other Threads of the same priority. Any attempt to yield to a Thread of lower priority is ignored.

Score: _____

Notes: _____

_____

37. The Thread class contains two constants that define the numeric values for the highest and lowest values for Thread priority. What are they?

Skill Level: Intermediate

Expected answer: They are `MIN_PRIORITY` and `MAX_PRIORITY`.

Score: _____

Notes: _____

_____

38. What is the name of the constant variable in the Thread class that holds the numeric value of the default priority assigned to a Thread?

Skill Level: Intermediate

Expected answer: `NORM_PRIORITY`

Score: _____

Notes: _____

_____

39. You have a class named MyThread that implements the Runnable interface. Write a sample code block that starts a Thread of type MyThread.

Skill Level: Intermediate

Expected answer:

```
Thread t1 = new Thread(new MyThread());
t1.start();
```

Make sure that the `MyThread` class has implemented the `run()` method since this is what `start()` will call.

Score: _____

Notes: _____

_____

40. You have an application that contains a separate Thread of control that is executing a long-running computation. What method could you call from within this computation that would suspend its operations, allowing the Thread scheduler to choose another runnable Thread to execute?

Skill Level: Intermediate

Expected answer: Within the long-running Thread, you would call the `yield()` method to suspend its operations, thus allowing other Threads a chance to run.

Score: _____

Notes: _____

_____

41. What is the difference between `sleep()` and `yield()`?

Skill Level: Intermediate

Expected answer: When a Thread calls the `sleep()` method, it will return to its *waiting state*. When a Thread calls the `yield()` method, it returns to the *ready state*.

Score: _____

Notes: _____

_____

42. Is the `yield()` method declared as a static method?

Skill Level: Intermediate

Expected answer: Yes.

Score: _____

Notes: _____

_____

43. If a Thread calls the `yield()` method, is it possible for the Thread scheduler to choose the same Thread that called the `yield()` method?

Skill Level: Intermediate

Expected answer: Yes, it is possible for the Thread scheduler to choose the same Thread that called the `yield()` method.

Score: _____

Notes: _____

_____

44. Say that, from within the `run()` method, you want to stop execution of the Thread by calling the `stop()` method from the Thread class. Is this safe to do?

Skill Level: Intermediate

Expected answer: No, the `stop()` method is now deprecated and should not be used. Although the method still exists, it should not be used as a technique for arbitrarily stopping a Thread as it may leave an object in a damaged or possibly inconsistent state. It is strongly advisable to exit from the `run()` method and stop the execution of the Thread .

45. What method of the Thread class would you use to check to see if a Thread has been interrupted without changing the *interrupted status* of the Thread?

Skill Level*:* Intermediate

Expected answer*:*

```
public Boolean isInterrupted()
```

Score:

Notes:

46. Is it possible to acquire a lock on a class?

Skill Level*:* Intermediate

Expected answer*:* Yes, it is possible to acquire a lock on a class. In this situation, a lock is acquired on the class's `Class` object.

Score:

Notes:

47. What is the state of a Thread when it blocks on I/O?

Skill Level: High

Expected answer: When a Thread blocks on I/O, it enters the wait state.

Score: _____

Notes: _____

_____

48. What is the initial state of a Thread after it is created and started?

Skill Level: High

Expected answer: After a Thread is created and started, it is in the ready state.

Score: _____

Notes: _____

_____

49. What happens to the status of the current Thread as it refers to its *interrupted status* when the `interrupted()` method has been called on it?

Skill Level: High

Expected answer: The `interrupted()` method is used to test whether the current Thread has been interrupted. But when this method is called, its interrupted status is cleared.

That means, if this method were to be called twice in succession, the second method call would return `false` (provided the current Thread were not interrupted again, after the first call had cleared its interrupted status and before the second call had examined it).

Score: _____

Notes: _____

_____

50. Say that, within your program, you used the `setPriority()` method to set your Thread to a particular priority. Later in the program, you call the `getPriority()` method, expecting to have returned the same value you specified when calling `setPriority()`. Is it possible for `getPriority` to return a different value from the one you requested, even if no one has made a manual change to the priority?

Skill Level: High

Expected answer: Yes, this is possible. In some cases, the JVM may have to adjust the priority downward to match the capabilities of the underlying operating system.

Score: _____

Notes: _____

_____

51. Is it possible to call the `wait()` method in a non-synchronized block?

Skill Level: High

Expected answer: No, it is not possible.

Score: _____

Notes: _____

_____

52. In a multithreaded application, must the method `generateIdNumber()` in the following code snippet be synchronized to ensure only unique numbers are returned, therefore guaranteeing Thread safety?

```
private static int nextIdNumber = 0;
public static int generateIdNumber() {
return nextIdNumber++;
}
```

Skill Level: High

Expected answer: Yes. At first glance, the return statement in the method only contains a single atomically writable action to change the state of the returned field (namely, `nextIdNumber`). However, the increment operator used (++) performs two actions: a `read` and then a `write` to the field; therefore, it is not atomic. The `read` and `write` methods are performed in sequence, independent of each other. It is possible for multiple concurrent Threads to read the current state of the field before the update (`write`), thus returning the same ID Number.

Score: _____

Notes: _____

_____

Java Collections Framework

1. What is the Java Collections Framework API?

   Skill Level: Low

   Expected answer: The Java Collection Framework API is a set of standard utility interfaces, classes, and algorithms that provide support for managing collections of objects.

   The framework provides for enhanced support to operate on groups of data throughout the life of your program. The framework also offers support that allows you to effortlessly separate data storage from data access.

   Score: _____

   Notes: _____

   _____

2. In what version of the Java SDK did the Java Collections Framework API first appear?

   Skill Level: Low

   Expected answer: Java 2 Standard Edition, version 1.2.

   Score: _____

   Notes: _____

   _____

3. How would you best define a collection?

   Skill Level: Low

   Expected answer: In a collection, a group of objects will be treated as a single object. The objects that are stored in a collection are then known as *elements* of that collection.

Score: _____

Notes: _____

_____

4. Which top-level interfaces in the Collection Framework API do not extend the Collection interface? Why?

Skill Level: Low

Expected answer: The `Map` interface (and `SortedMap`) does not extend the `Collection` interface. A map is not a collection. Maps do not contain elements, but rather contain *mappings* (sometimes called *entries*). Mappings are a set of key = value pairs.

Score: _____

Notes: _____

_____

5. In which package would you find the interfaces and classes defined in the Java Collections Framework?

Skill Level: Low

Expected answer: `java.util`

Score: _____

Notes: _____

_____

6. What two methods defined in the Collection interface allow you to add elements to a collection?

Skill Level: Low

Expected answer: The methods are:

`add()` — Adds an element to a collection.

`addAll()` — Adds a collection of elements to a collection.

Score: _____

Notes: _____

_____

7. What method defined in the Collection interface allows you to determine the current size of the collection? (E.g. How many elements are in the collection?)

Skill Level: Low

Expected answer: The `size()` method returns an `int` value indicating the number of elements in the collection.

Score: _____

Notes: _____

_____

8. What method in the Collection interface can tell you whether or not the collection is empty?

Skill Level: Low

Expected answer: The `isEmpty()` method returns the Boolean value `true` if the collection is empty and `false` otherwise.

Score: _____

Notes: _____

_____

9. Java 2 includes two special classes in the Collections Framework that consists of many static methods for working with and manipulating collection instances. What are the names of these two classes, and in which package can they be found?

Expected answer: The two special classes are `Collections` and `Arrays`. Both are found in the `java.util` package.

Score: _____

Notes: _____

_____

10. What is the difference between Java's historical collections (i.e., Vector, Stack, Hashtable, Dictionary, Bitset, and so on) and the new collections found in the Java 2 Collections Framework as it relates to Thread safety and synchronization?

Skill Level: Low

Expected answer: The historical collections are Thread safe by default, whether you need this feature or not. None of the new collections in the Java 2 Collections Framework are Thread safe.

Score: _____

Notes: _____

_____

11. If you need Thread safety when working with collections in the Java 2 Collections Framework, what methods are available in the Collections class to provide for implementations that are Thread safe (List, Set, Map, and so on)?

Skill Level: Low

Expected answer: The `Collections` class provides several methods that allow you to create implementations of the new collections that are Thread safe. Here are two examples that create a `Map`, `List`, and `Set` object with a size of 50:

```
Map map =
Collections.synchronizedMap(new HashMap(50));

List list =
Collections.synchronizedList(new ArrayList(50));

Set set =
Collections.synchronizedSet(new HashSet(50));
```

Score: _____

Notes: _____

_____

12. Say that you created a HashSet object named mySet using:

```
Set set =
Collections.synchronizedSet(new        HashSet(50));
```

You now need to walk through the set using an Iterator. Is the Iterator Thread safe? If not, how would you traverse the set in a Thread-safe manner?

Skill Level: High

Expected answer: The `Iterator` is not synchronized and is therefore not Thread safe. When iterating through a collection, the `Iterator` must make multiple calls back to the collection, and these calls are not atomic. Therefore, the underlying elements in the collection may change. Here is an example of how to walk through the previously-created collection in a Thread-safe manner:

```
Set set =
Collections.synchronizedSet(new HashSet(50));
synchronized(set) {
Iterator i = set.iterator();
while (i.hasNext()) {
System.out.println(i.next());
}
}
```

Score: _____

Notes: _____

_____

13. What is the one basic collection used in many programs and built right into the Java programming language?

Skill Level: Low

Expected answer: The collection is Array.

Score: _____

Notes: _____

_____

14. In Java, at what index value do Arrays start?

Skill Level: Low

Expected answer: Arrays start at zero.

Score: _____

Notes: _____

_____

15. Is it possible to set the length variable of an array to increase and decrease the size of an array?

Skill Level: Low

Expected answer: No, this is not possible. There is no way to modify the size of an array once it is created. The length variable is only used to determine what is an array's upper boundary.

Score: _____

Notes: _____

_____

16. What class and method provided in the Java API are used to sort an array?

Skill Level: Low

Expected answer: Use the `sort()` method available in the `java.util.Arrays` class. Assuming you have an array named `myArray`, here is how you would sort the array:

```
Arrays.sort(myArray);
```

Score: _____

Notes: _____

_____

17. What method in the System class allows you to copy elements from one array to another?

Skill Level: Low

Expected answer: Use the `arraycopy()` static method available in the `System` class. Here is the signature of the `arraycopy()` method:

```
public static void arraycopy(Object src
, int    srcPos
, Object dest
, int    destPos
, int    length)
```

Score: _____

Notes: _____

_____

18. When using the `System.arraycopy()` method, what exception is thrown if the destination array is smaller than the source array?

Skill Level: Low

Expected answer: If the destination array is smaller than the source array, an `ArrayIndexOutOfBoundsException` will be thrown at runtime.

Score: _____

Notes: _____

_____

19. When using the `System.arraycopy()` method, will an exception be thrown if the destination array is larger than the source array?

Skill Level: Low

Expected answer: No exception will be thrown. The destination array can be larger than the source array. However, the source array cannot be larger than the destination array.

Score: _____

Notes: _____

_____

20. Consider a Boolean array in which none of the entries in the array have been initialized. What is the default value for each value of the array?

Skill Level: Low

Expected answer: The default value is `false`.

Score: _____

Notes: _____

_____

21. Write a one-line Java statement that declares, constructs, and initializes an integer (int) array named array1 with the values 3, 4, and 5?

Skill Level: Intermediate

Expected answer:

```
int array1[] = {3,4,5};
```

Score: _____

Notes: _____

_____

22. Is a character array the same as a String object in Java?

Skill Level: Intermediate

Expected answer: No. Unlike languages like C and C++, character arrays in Java are not String objects. Keep in mind that within Java, it is easy to convert between the two using the String constructor, but they are certainly different.

Score: _____

Notes: _____

_____

23. What is the Vector class?

Skill Level: Intermediate

Expected answer: The `Vector` class is one of Java's historical collections that provide the capabilities to implement a *growable* array of objects.

Arrays are good when you know the size of your collection and when all the elements of the collection are of the same type. The `Vector` class provides a practical solution to the aforementioned limitations in arrays by providing you with a dynamically sized data structure able to store any object (but not primitives).

Score: _____

Notes: _____

_____

24. Using a Vector, what method would you call to change the size of the internal vector buffer?

Skill Level: Intermediate

Expected answer:

```
public setSize(int newSize)
```

Score: _____

Notes: _____

_____

25. When using the `setSize()` method of the Vector class, what happens if you set the size of the collection to a size smaller than the number of elements in the Vector?

Skill Level: High

Expected answer: The `Vector` drops off elements from the end.

26. In the Vector class, what does the `capacity()` method tell you?

    Skill Level: High

    Expected answer: The `capacity()` method of the `Vector` class returns the number of elements a vector can hold before it needs to resize any of its internal data structures. Its signature is:

    ```
    public int capacity()
    ```

27. What are the only two methods defined in the Enumeration interface?

    Skill Level: Intermediate

    Expected answer:

    `hasMoreElements()` — Checks to see if there are more elements in the enumeration.

    `nextElement()` — Fetches the next element in the enumeration.

28. The Enumeration interface is one of Java's historical interfaces. Which interface, introduced in Java 2, version 1.2, replaces the Enumeration interface and provides for several new capabilities for traversing collections?

Skill Level*:* Intermediate

Expected answer*:* The `Iterator` interface was added to the Collections Framework (Java 2, version 1.2) to replace the `Enumeration` interface.

Score: _____

Notes: _____

_____

29. What is the Iterator interface?

Skill Level*:* Intermediate

Expected answer*:* The `Iterator` interface is implemented by all collections to provide a means to sequentially step through and access the elements in a collection. This `Iterator` replaced the `Enumeration` interface in Java 2, version 1.2.

Score: _____

Notes: _____

_____

30. What are the three methods in the Iterator interface and what do they do?

Skill Level*:* Intermediate

Expected answer*:* The `Iterator` interface has three methods:

`hasNext()` — Returns `true` if the iteration has more elements.
`next()` — Returns the next element in the iteration.

`remove()` — Removes the last element returned by the `Iterator` from the underlying collection.

Score: _____

Notes: _____

_____

31. What is the **List** interface?

Skill Level: Low

Expected answer: The `List` interface extends the `Collection` interface and is used to maintain an ordered sequence of elements. The elements in a `List` are ordered by their position (index value) in the list.

Score: _____

Notes: _____

_____

32. Is it possible for a List object to contain object references of more than one type?

Skill Level: Intermediate

Expected answer: Yes

Score: _____

Notes: _____

_____

33. What are some of the concrete implementations of the List interface?

Skill Level: Low

Expected answer: Within the Java Collections Framework, there are `ArrayList` and `LinkedList`.

Two other historical collections exist; they are `Vector` and `Stack`.

Score: _____

Notes: _____

_____

34. What is the name of the Iterator that you should use for a List to traverse the elements in both directions?

Skill Level: Intermediate

Expected answer: The iterator is `ListIterator`.

Score: _____

Notes: _____

_____

35. What are the capabilities provided with the ListIterator interface that are not available with the Iterator when using a List collection?

Skill Level: Intermediate

Expected answer: The `ListIterator` has capabilities beyond the normal `Iterator` when working with a `List` collection. For example, you can traverse the list in either direction, modify the list during iteration, and obtain the `iterator's` current position in the list

Score: _____

Notes: _____

_____

36. Say you are about to insert a considerable number of elements into an `ArrayList`. What method, although not required, should be called to ensure the elements you are about to add

will not cause an excessive number of resizes of the internal data structures during insertion time?

Skill Level: High

Expected answer: You can use the `ensureCapacity(minimumCapacity)` method to increase the capacity of the `ArrayList` instance. The `minimumCapacity` argument is an `int` value. It indicates the size (number of elements) of the internal data structures to which the ArrayList should be sized.

Score: _____

Notes: _____

_____

37. After adding all of the elements you need to the ArrayList collection, what method could you use to reduce the amount of unused space within the internal data structures?

Skill Level: High

Expected answer: You should use the `trimToSize()` method.

Score: _____

Notes: _____

_____

38. If you try to add or remove an element from a list that does not support adding or removing elements, what exception is thrown in both operation attempts?

Skill Level: Intermediate

Expected answer: The `UnsupportedOperationException` is thrown when you attempt to add or remove an element from a list that does not support those operations.

Score: _____

Notes: _____

_____

39. Is the LinkedList implementation provided by the Collection Framework a doubly linked list?

Skill Level: Low

Expected answer: Yes. The `LinkedList` implementation internally maintains references to the previous and next element at each node in the list.

Score: _____

Notes: _____

_____

40. What are the two methods in the LinkedList implementation that allow you to treat the linked list as either a *queue* or a *stack* data structure for adding elements?

Skill Level: High

Expected answer: To treat the linked list as a *queue* data structure, you would use the `addLast(Object element)` method. To use the linked list as a *stack* data structure, you would use the `addFirst(Object element)`.

Score: _____

Notes: _____

_____

41. What is the Map interface?

Skill Level: Intermediate

Expected answer: The `Map` interface is included in the Java Collections Framework, but unlike all other interfaces, does not extend from the `Collection` interface. The `Map` interface is the root of its own hierarchy and replaces the historical `Dictionary` class. Maps do not contain elements, but rather contain mappings (sometimes called entries). Mappings are a set of key = value pairs. Given some key value, the map obtains its value.

Score: _____

Notes: _____

_____

42. What are the four concrete implementation of the Map interface?

Skill Level: Low

Expected answer: The four concrete implementations are `HashMap`, `WeakHashMap`, `TreeMap`, and `Hashtable`. Keep in mind that the `Hashtable` implementation is part of Java's historical collection.

Score: _____

Notes: _____

_____

43. Consider the following code snippet:

```
Map myMap = new HashMap();
myMap.put("key", "String1");
myMap.put("key", "String2");
```

How many values will be stored in the map and what are they after executing this code block?

Skill Level: Intermediate

Expected answer: After the code block executes, only one value will be stored in the map with the string value `String2`. When you attempt to add a value to the map with the same key, the new value replaces the old value. In the case of this example, the value `String2` replaces the value `String1`.

Score: _____

Notes: _____

_____

44. What is the Set interface?

Skill Level: Intermediate

Expected answer: The `Set` interface corresponds to a group of elements without duplicates and that have no perceivable order. (There are, however, specific implementations that do provide order.) Nothing defined in the interface forces the collection not to have duplicates. This definition is enforced in the actual implementations.

Score: _____

Notes: _____

_____

45. What are some of the concrete implementations of the Set interface?

Skill Level: Low

Expected answer: Within the Java Collections Framework, you have `TreeSet` and `HashSet`.

Score: _____

Notes: _____

_____

46. Which of the Set implementations support an ordered collection?

Skill Level: Intermediate

Expected answer: The `TreeSet` supports ordering. The `TreeSet` collection works much in the same way as the `HashSet`, but supports its elements to be ordered internally.

Score: _____

Notes: _____

_____

47. Does the TreeSet collection maintain a balanced tree?

Skill Level: Intermediate

Expected answer: Yes, internally, the `TreeSet` maintains a balanced tree.

Score: _____

Notes: _____

_____

48. The TreeSet implementation maintains a balanced tree. What is its guaranteed search time, expressed in Big-O notation?

Skill Level: High

Expected answer: O(log n)

Score: _____

Notes: _____

_____

49. What collection is used as the "backend" data structure for the HashSet collection for storing its unique elements?

Skill Level: Intermediate

Expected answer: The `HashSet` implementation uses a `HashMap` as its backend data structure for storing unique elements. The implementation only uses the *key* component of the `HashMap` while storing a dummy string for its value.

Score: _____

Notes: _____

_____

50. What is the default *load factor* for a HashSet collection? Can you specify another load factor when creating the collection?

Skill Level: Intermediate

Expected answer: The default load factor is 75%. Yes, you can specify another custom load factor value by using the following constructor:

```
public HashSet(int initialCapacity, int loadFactor);
```

Score: _____

Notes: _____

_____

Java I/O

1. Which package in the Java API includes a collection of stream classes that support algorithms for reading and writing I/O streams?

   Skill Level: Low

   Expected answer: `java.io`

   Score: _____

   Notes: _____

   _____

2. The Java I/O stream classes are divided into two basic class hierarchies. What are they?

   Skill Level: Low

   Expected answer: The two stream classes are byte streams and character streams.

   Score: _____

   Notes: _____

   _____

3. What are the names of the two abstract superclasses for reading and writing all character streams in the `java.io` package?

   Skill Level: Low

   Expected answer: `Reader` and `Writer`.

   Score: _____

   Notes: _____

   _____

4. Would it be best to use a *Reader* or an *Input Stream* to read in textual information?

   Skill Level: Low

   Expected answer: You should use a *Reader* since it can handle any character in the Unicode character set, whereas byte streams are limited to ISO-Latin-1 8-bit bytes.

   Score: _____

   Notes: _____

   _____

5. What is the length (in bits) of each character read and written using the character streaming classes?

   Skill Level: Low

   Expected answer: The length of each is 16 bits.

   Score: _____

   Notes: _____

   _____

6. Which character set do the character stream classes use?

   Skill Level: Low

   Expected answer: Character stream classes use the Unicode character set.

   Score: _____

   Notes: _____

   _____

7. Which character set do the byte stream classes use?

   Skill Level: Low

   Expected answer: Byte stream classes use ISO-Latin-1 8-bit bytes.

   Score: _____

   Notes: _____

   _____

8. What is the size (in bits) of all Unicode characters?

   Skill Level: Low

   Expected answer: All Unicode characters are 16 bits.

   Score: _____

   Notes: _____

   _____

9. What is printed out as a result of the following code snippet?

   ```
   File file = new File("/u01/app/oracle");
   System.out.println(file.getParent());
   ```

   Skill Level: Low

   Expected answer: /u01/app

   Score: _____

   Notes: _____

   _____

10. For any of the steam classes (reader, writer, input streams, and output streams), if you do not explicitly call the close() method to the stream, what process will eventually close the stream for you?

    Skill Level: Intermediate

Expected answer: It is possible for the programmer to explicitly call the `close()` method for a stream, but if you choose not to close the stream explicitly, the *garbage collector* will implicitly close it for you when the object is no longer referenced.

Score: _____

Notes: _____

_____

11. Say you are reading and writing binary streams. Which two streams (reading/writing) could be used with other streams to reduce the number of accesses on the original data, thereby improving reading and writing efficiency? What two streams would you use if you were reading/writing character streams?

Skill Level: Intermediate

Expected answer: For binary streams, you would use a `BufferedInputStream` for reading and a `BufferedOutputStream` for writing. These streams are typically used with other streams to reduce the number of access calls to the original data, thereby increasing efficiency.

For character streams, you would use the `BufferedReader` and `BufferedWriter` streams.

Score: _____

Notes: _____

_____

12. Which two stream classes would you use to serialize (read/write) objects?

Skill Level: Intermediate

Expected answer: The `ObjectInputStream` and `ObjectOutputStream` handle object serialization.

Score: _____

Notes: _____

_____

13. When reading from a stream, it is sometimes useful to peek at the next few characters or bytes in the stream to decide what to do next. Which streams (character and binary) can be used to perform this?

Skill Level: High

Expected answer: For character streams, use `PushbackReader`, and for binary streams, use `PushbackInputStream`.

Score: _____

Notes: _____

_____

14. Suppose you want to create a single stream from multiple input sources. This comes in handy when you want to implement a concatenation utility that sequentially concatenates several files together. Which stream class provided in the java.io package would you use to easily perform this?

Skill Level: High

Expected answer: You would use the `SequenceInputStream` class.

Score: _____

Notes: _____

_____

15. How do you delete a file in Java?

Skill Level: Low

Expected answer: Use the `delete()` method from the `java.io.File` package.

Score: _____

Notes: _____

_____

16. Does object serialization require that the ObjectInputStream and ObjectOutputStream be constructed from different streams?

Skill Level: Low

Expected answer: Yes. For example, if you were serializing to and from a file, you would construct the `ObjectInputStream` using a `FileInputStream` while constructing an `ObjectOutputStream` would use a `FileOutputStream`.

Score: _____

Notes: _____

_____

17. What interface must a class implement before it can be serialized?

Skill Level: Low

Expected answer: There are two possible answers to this question. The first and most common solution is to implement the `java.io.Serializable` interface, which has no methods. The other way to enable a class to be serialized is to implement the `Externalizable` interface, which defines two methods. This method is only used when you need to provide special requirements.

Score: _____

Notes: _____

_____

18. What is *Object serialization?*

Skill Level*:* Intermediate

Expected answer*: Object serialization* is a powerful feature introduced in Java 1.1 that provides a program with the ability to read or write an entire object to and from a RAW byte stream. With this feature, you can encode Java objects and primitives into a byte stream suitable for streaming to some type of network, file system, database column, or more generally, to a transmission medium or storage facility.

Score: _____

Notes: _____

_____

19. What are the two main purposes of using *object serialization?*

Skill Level*:* Intermediate

Expected answer*: Object serialization* is used:

- to a large extent, within the RMI API as a means for clients and servers to exchange objects.

- when developers need to save a specific object to disk and want to recreate that object at some later point in time.

Score: _____

Notes: _____

_____

20. Is it possible to find the creation date of a file using pure Java?

Skill Level: Intermediate

Expected answer: As of the Java SDK 1.4, this is not possible. Java may add this to their specification in future releases, but as of now, it is not possible to find a file's creation date. The reason the API does not include a method for retrieving the creation date is that not all file systems store the date a file was created.

The only thing that you can achieve in pure Java is to retrieve the last modified date, which may or may not be its creation date.

If it is a requirement to retrieve the creation date of a file, you may be able to use JNI and some "hacked up" code using Runtime.exec(), but this would make your code less portable.

Score: _____

Notes: _____

_____

21. Is there a way to get a list of all files in the current working directory using the File class? If so, sketch out a code snippet that would perform this.

Skill Level: Intermediate

Expected answer: Yes, this is possible. Here is a sample code snippet that performs this:

```
File f = new File(".");
String[] files = f.list();
for (int i=0; i < files.length; i++) {
System.out.println(files[i]);
}
```

Score: _____

Notes: _____

_____

22. Do readers have methods for reading and returning primitive data types like float, int, double?

Skill Level: Intermediate

Expected answer: No, readers and writers can only deal with character I/O.

Score: _____

Notes: _____

_____

23. Consider running the following statement in an empty directory:

```
File f = new ("file.txt");
```

Will the file be created, since it doesn't exist?

Skill Level: Intermediate

Expected answer: No; simply constructing the class has no effect on creating the file on the file system.

Score: _____

Notes: _____

_____

24. In the File (String x, String y) constructor, what do both of the parameters stand for?

Skill Level: Intermediate

Expected answer: The first parameter, x in this case, is the file's parent directory name. The second parameter, y in this case, is the name of the file.

Score: _____

Notes: _____

_____

25. What value is returned from the `readLine()` method when it has reached the end of a file?

Skill Level: Intermediate

Expected answer: The value returned is `null`.

Score: _____

Notes: _____

_____

26. What value is returned from the `read()` method when it has reached the end of a file?

Skill Level: Intermediate

Expected answer: The value returned is `-1`.

Score: _____

Notes: _____

_____

27. For what are the DataInputStream and DataOutputStream classes used?

Skill Level: High

Expected answer: The `DataOutputStream`, a subclass of `FilterOutputStream`, is used to write Java primitive types to an output stream in a portable way. A `DataInputStream`, a subclass of `FilterInputStream`, provides an application with the ability to read Java primitive types from an underlying input stream in a portable (machine independent) way.

Both streams represent Unicode strings in an encoding format similar to UTF-8.

Score: _____

Notes: _____

_____

28. In which package would you find the ZipInputStream and ZipOutputStream classes?

Skill Level: High

Expected answer: You would find them in the `java.util.zip` package.

Score: _____

Notes: _____

_____

29. Which two streams can be used to keep track of line numbers while reading?

Skill Level: High

Expected answer: For character streams, you can use `LineNumberReader`; for binary streams, use `LineNumberInputStream`.

Score: _____

Notes: _____

_____

30. What is an I/O filter?

Skill Level: High

Expected answer: The `java.io` package contains several I/O filter classes. The I/O filter classes provide an object with the means to read from one stream and write to another while altering the data in some way (depending on the implementation of the I/O filter class) as it is passed from one stream to the other.

Score: _____

Notes: _____

_____

Conducting the Java Job Interview

Java Networking

1. Which package in the Java API contains interfaces and classes for network communication programming?

    Skill Level: Low

    Expected answer: The `java.net` package contains these interfaces and classes.

    Score: _____

    Notes: _____

    _____

2. What is the name of the class in the java.net package that can be used to represent an *Internet Protocol (IP) Address*?

    Skill Level: Low

    Expected answer: The class is `InetAddress`.

    Score: _____

    Notes: _____

    _____

3. Which class in the java.net package would you use if you need to represent an *Internet Protocol (IP) Version 6 Address*?

    Skill Level: Low

    Expected answer: You would use `Inet6Address`.

    Score: _____

    Notes: _____

    _____

4. What is the purpose of the ServerSocket class and in what package is it found?

Skill Level: Intermediate

Expected answer: This class is used to generate objects that set up connections on a server by implementing *server sockets*. A server socket will wait for requests to come in over a network. It will perform some operations based on that request, and then possibly return a result to the requestor. Keep in mind that the actual work of the server socket is performed by an instance of the SocketImpl class.

The ServerSocket class can be found in the **java.net** package.

Score: _____

Notes: _____

_____

5. For what is the URL class used? In which package is it located?

Skill Level: Intermediate

Expected answer: The java.net.URL class is used to represent a *Uniform Resource Locator (URL)*. A URL is an address that serves as a pointer to a resource on the World Wide Web. A resource can be something as simple as a file or directory, or as complex as a reference to a database query. Java programs will use the URL class to represent the URL address; for example, to find resources on the Internet that they wish to access.

The URL string has two main parts: the protocol needed to access the resource and the location of the resource. Here is an example URL that uses the HTTP protocol to retrieve the resource index.html from host java.sun.com.

```
http://java.sun.com/index.html
```

The URL class is found in the package **java.net**.

Score: _____

Notes: _____

_____

6. What are some of the protocols that can be defined in a URL?

Skill Level: Low

Expected answer: The protocols are http, ftp, gopher, news.

Score: _____

Notes: _____

_____

7. Given the URL http://www.acme.com, how would you turn this absolute URI into a URL object?

Skill Level: Low

Expected answer: First create a URI object, then use the to URL() method to return a URL object. The following code provides an example:

```
try {
URI uri = new URI("http://www.acme.com");
URL url = uri.toURL();
}
catch (URISyntaxException e) {}
catch (IllegalArgumentException e) {}
catch (MalformedURLException e) {}
```

8. Given the URL http://www.acme.com, how would you turn this URL into a URI object?

   Skill Level: Intermediate

   Expected answer: First create a URL object, then use the toString() method to create a String object that can be used as an argument to instantiate a new URI object. The following code provides an example:

```
try {
URL url = new URL("http://www.acme.com");
URI uri = new URI(url.toString());
}
catch (URISyntaxException e) {}
catch (IllegalArgumentException e) {}
catch (MalformedURLException e) {}
```

9. When creating a URL object using the constructor listed below, what value would you specify as the *port number* to indicate that the URL should use the default port for the protocol?

```
public URL(String protocol,
String host,
int port,
String file)
```

   Skill Level: Low

   Expected answer: Passing in a value of -1 for the port number indicates that the URL object should be created using the default port number for the passed-in protocol. For example, if the protocol being passed in is *HTTP*, then passing in a -1 for the port number will create a URL object with a port value of 80.

Score: _____

Notes: _____

_____

10. What is the default port for an HTTP (Web) server?

Skill Level: Low

Expected answer: The default is Port 80.

Score: _____

Notes: _____

_____

11. What are the methods that you can use to retrieve the protocol, host, port, file, and reference of a URL object named URL?

Skill Level: Intermediate

Expected answer:

```
String protocol = url.getProtocol();
String host     = url.getHost();
String port     = url.getPort();
String file     = url.getFile();
String ref      = url.getRef();
```

Score: _____

Notes: _____

_____

12. What is the difference between a *port* and a *socket?*

Skill Level: Intermediate

Expected answer: A *port* is a unique, two-byte number (16 bits) used as a software address for a computer on a network. There can be 65535 ports on a computer. A port can be thought of as a conduit into your computer where data flows. It is important to understand that a port is not a hardware concept. It is a network abstraction that enables programmers to easily develop programs that read data from and write data to a network. Here are some well-known port numbers on a TCP/IP-based network:

Port #	Facility	Description
7	ECHO	Echoes back anything sent
13	DAYTIME	Gives the time of day
21	FTP	File Transfer Protocol
23	TELNET	Remote terminal access
80	HTTP	HTTP Web Server

On a TCP/IP based computer, the unique pair of numbers consisting of the IP address and the port number identifies each communication channel. This combination of IP address and port number is a programming abstraction known as a socket. Sockets are software endpoints for communication between two machines, and subsequently, between programs that use Internet protocols. A socket can be thought of as a communications path to a port for a given application. Java developers who want their programs to communicate over the network must give the programs a way of addressing the port. They can do this by creating a socket and attaching it to the port. A socket is responsible for accepting data at the specified port and delivering it to the program/application.

13. What does *reverse name resolution* mean?

    Skill Level: Intermediate

    Expected answer: Using *reverse name resolution* for any IP address, causes the host associated with the IP address to be returned.

    Score: _____

    Notes: _____

    _____

14. How would you perform *reverse name resolution* to return a machine's host name if you have a textual representation of a machine's IP address?

    Skill Level: High

    Expected answer: You would first pass in the textual representation of the machine's IP address to the `InetAddress.getByName()` method. Then, call either the `getHostName()` or `getCanonicalHostName()` method. Here is an example:

```
InetAddress inetAddress = null;

// Get the host name given textual
// representation of the IP address
try {
inetAddress = InetAddress.getByName(ipAddress);
} catch (UnknownHostException e) {}
// Get machine's host name
System.out.println(inetAddress.getHostName());

// Get machine's canonical host name
System.out.println(inetAddress.getCanonicalHostName());
```

Score: _____

Notes: _____

_____

15. If you pass a textual representation of an IP address to the getByName() method, what is returned by the method getHostName() if the method is not able to resolve the IP address to a host name?

Skill Level: Low

Expected answer: If the getByName() cannot resolve the IP address to a host name, the getHostName() method will simply return the original passed-in IP address.

Score: _____

Notes: _____

_____

16. What method in the InetAddress class can be used to create an InetAddress object of the local host?

Skill Level: Low

Expected answer: The InetAddress class includes a static method called getLocalHost() that can be used to return a InetAddress object of the local host. Here is an example of using the getLocalHost() method:

```
try {
InetAddress inet = InetAddress.getLocalHost();
} catch (UnknownHostException e) {}
```

Score: _____

Notes: _____

_____

17. What is the default implementation and form of the returned String of the `toString()` method in the `InetAddress` class?

Skill Level: Low

Expected answer: The `String` returned by the `toString()` of the `InetAddress` class is of the form:

hostname / literal IP address

It is important to understand that the `toString()` method does not attempt to reverse name resolution of any unresolved host names. If the host name is not resolved, the hostname part will be represented by an empty string.

Score: _____

Notes: _____

_____

18. When using the `getByName()` method to create an `InetAddress` object for the *local host*, what should be passed to the `getByName()` method?

Skill Level: Low

Expected answer: What should be passed is `null`. Here is an example call to the `getByName()` method to return an `InetAddress` representing the local host:

```
try {
InetAddress inet = InetAddress.getByName(null);
} catch (UnknownHostException e) {}
```

Score: _____

Notes: _____

_____

19. When using the `getByName()` method to create an `InetAddress` object, what exception must you catch if the host name passed in cannot be resolved to an IP address?

Skill Level: Low

Expected answer: You must catch the `UnknownHostException`. Here is an example that throws an `UnknownHostException` exception:

```
try {
InetAddress inet =
InetAddress.getByName("machine.noresolve");
} catch (UnknownHostException e) {}
```

Score: _____

Notes: _____

_____

20. What class is typically used to create a client socket?

Skill Level: Low

Expected answer: The class is Socket.

Score: _____

Notes: _____

_____

21. Say you've created a client Socket object named socket. What method would you use to return an InetAddress object that represents the address to which it is connected?

Skill Level: Low

Expected answer: You would use the `getInetAddress()` of the `Socket` class as follows:

```
InetAddress ia = sock.getInetAddress();
```

22. What is meant by the term, "well-known ports" of a computer and what is their range of addresses?

Skill Level: Intermediate

Expected answer: Well-known ports are port numbers that are assigned to specific applications by the IANA. A range of well-known port numbers is one on which well-known services such as Mail (SMTP), POP, FTP, HTTP, and TELNET run. Custom programs you write should not normally use these ports.

Its address number range is $0 - 1023$.

23. What is the difference between the two transport protocol socket classes ServerSocket and DatagramSocket?

Skill Level: High

Expected answer: The DatagramSocket class is designed for UDP communication, while ServerSocket is used for TCP. Neither of these transport protocols can be ranked as better or worse. It all depends on the application and the tasks you need to perform.

TCP is a very reliable communication stream in that it ensures order and delivery of packets while UDP does not. However, UDP packets are much smaller, given that they don't have large header sizes like those found in TCP packets. Since UDP packets are smaller, they will probably arrive at their destination faster than TCP packets. UDP is typically used when you do care about retransmission or packet order. Sending and receiving sound is an example of an application that should use UDP. With sound, it is better to make small pauses on missing packets rather than to play a particular packet out of order. In short, if you do not mind losing small pieces of data, use UDP. Otherwise, use TCP.

Score: _____

Notes: _____

_____

24. Is it possible to *ping* an email address?

Skill Level: High

Expected answer: No; if this were possible, spammers would have a field day detecting valid email addresses to use as their target. Spammers would be able to create a simple loop that would be able to detect valid email addresses with AOL and other well-known domains in a very short matter of time. It is possible, however, to create a simple Java method that validates the format of an email address. This method can even go as far as to ping the domain at the right of the email address, although it does not always work. The only way to validate an email address is to post a message to it.

Score: _____

Notes: _____

_____

25. What is *nagling*, and how do you turn it on and off in Java?

Skill Level: High

Expected answer: Named after John Nagle, *nagling* is a network transmission algorithm that specifies a means of dealing with what he called the small packet problem. This problem occurs when someone tries to send, for example, one character over the network. Sending only one byte will add an additional ~40 bytes to the packet for header information. Sending one page of text with small packets will cause enormous overhead.

The nagle algorithm avoids this overhead trouble and only sends packets when they become large enough to send.

In some applications, however, you may want to send one byte of code anyway; for example, an application that sends a heart beat to a production server. To disable nagling, use the setTcpNoDelay(true) class from the java.net.Socket package.

Score: _____

Notes: _____

_____

Java Swing/AWT

1. **Swing** is only one component of a group of features called the Java Foundation Classes (JFC) used for building graphical user interfaces. What are some of the other features included in the JFC?

   Skill Level: Low

   Expected answer: Some of the other features are:

   - Pluggable look and feel
   - Accessibility API
   - Java 2D API (Java 2 platform only)
   - Drag and drop support (Java 2 platform only)

   Score: _____

   Notes: _____

   _____

2. In what version of the Java SDK did Sun start to include the Swing API as a core part of the product?

   Skill Level: Low

   Expected answer: Java SDK 1.2

   Score: _____

   Notes: _____

   _____

3. What is the name of the design pattern that Java uses for all Swing components?

   Skill Level: Low

Expected answer: All Swing components use a slight variant of the Model / View / Controller (MVC) design known as *model-delegate*. This design unites the View and the Controller elements into a single element known as the *UI delegate*. The UI delegate is responsible for drawing the component to the screen and handling GUI events. The model communicates with the UI delegate in a bi-directional manner.

Score: _____

Notes: _____

_____

4. Briefly describe each of the three elements of the Model / View / Controller (MVC) design pattern?

Skill Level: Low

Expected answer:

Model

The model component comprises the state data and other low-level information for each component. The model has no specific knowledge of the components' View or Controller elements. With this pattern, the system itself maintains links between the model and views and notifies the views when the model changes state.

Each component is capable of storing different types of state information, depending on the component itself. Take, for example a scrollbar component. The scrollbar model will store information about its current position, width, and maximum and minimum possible values. The model data is always independent of the visual representation of how the component is painted to the screen.

View

The view element is associated with how you see the component on the screen. The view element uses the state information represented in the model. Consider what an application window looks like on two different GUI platforms. Most frames have a title bar that spans the top of the window and generally has a Close button. On Mac OS, the Close button is located on the left of the title bar, and in Windows, this button is located on the right side of the title bar. Even the scrollbar example used previously will look different on different GUI platforms.

Controller

The controller is used to manage user interaction with the model element. It dictates how the component interacts with events (i.e., mouse clicks, keyboard events, gaining or loosing focus, or even a directive to repaint part of the screen). The controller provides the means by which changes are made to the state information of the model.

To summarize, the model passes its data (state information) to the view for rendering. The view establishes which events are passed to the controller. The controller then updates the model based on the events it receives from the view.

Score: _____

Notes: _____

_____

5. In what package would you find most of the AWT events that support the event-delegation model?

Skill Level: Low

Expected answer: The `java.awt.event` package contains most of the interfaces and classes for dealing with different types of events fired by AWT components.

Score: _____

Notes: _____

_____

6. What is the purpose of the `pack()` method found in the java.awt.Window package?

Skill Level: Low

Expected answer: The `pack()` method uses its layout manager to size a window to fit the preferred size and layouts of its subcomponents.

It is important to understand that the `pack()` method uses a layout manager to control the size of the window; you should not use this method if you don't have a layout manager (like the one used in absolute positioning).

In many references, you will see arguments on both sides about whether or not to use `setSize()` or `pack()`. Neither argument is absolutely right or wrong. The developer must decide whether to use exact dimensions for the window using `setSize()` or the automatic `pack()` method.

Score: _____

Notes: _____

_____

7. What is the height and width of a newly constructed JFrame if neither the `pack()` method or the `setSize()` is called?

   Skill Level: Low

   Expected answer: Height = 0 and Width = 0.

   Score: _____

   Notes: _____

   _____

8. What method must be called on a newly constructed JFrame to make it visible?

   Skill Level: Low

   Expected answer: `setVisible(true);`

   Score: _____

   Notes: _____

   _____

9. When attempting to close the main application frame, the default implementation is to hide the frame. This causes the virtual machine to continue running a frame that is not visible. What new method is included with the Java SDK 1.4 that allows you to exit the application when the JFrame is closed?

   Skill Level: Low

   Expected answer: The new method is:

   ```
   setDefaultCloseOperation(JFrame.EXIT_ON_CLOSE);
   ```

   Score: _____

   Notes: _____

   _____

10. What is a Top-Level Container?

Skill Level: Low

Expected answer: Any Java application that utilizes Swing components requires at least one *top-level container*. When working with Swing, all Swing components in the GUI (JPanel, JButton, JLabel, and so on) fit into one or more *containment hierarchies*. All containment hierarchies have at their root a *top-level container*. A top-level container exists mainly to provide a placeholder for other Swing components to paint themselves to the screen.

Useful, top-level containers are JFrame, JDialog, and JApplet. JWindow is another top-level container, but is not used very often.

Score: _____

Notes: _____

_____

11. What are the three generally useful top-level containers included with Swing?

Skill Level: Low

Expected answer: They are JFrame, JDialog, and JApplet.

There is a fourth top-level container called JWindow, but it is not used very often. A JWindow container is nothing more than a Swing version of the AWT Window class that provides a window with no controls or title. It is always on top of the every other window.

Also note that JInternalFrame is not a top-level container, but rather is considered to be an intermediate container.

Score: _____

Notes: _____

_____

12. For a standalone application with a Swing-based GUI, what is the top-level container at the root used in the containment hierarchy?

Skill Level: Low

Expected answer: `JFrame`

Score: _____

Notes: _____

_____

13. What special intermediate container does every top-level container have that is used to contain the visible components in the top-level container's GUI?

Skill Level: Low

Expected answer: This is the content pane.

Score: _____

Notes: _____

_____

14. Suppose you have a JFrame object named frame. What method would you use to get the frame's content pane?

Skill Level: Low

Expected answer: The method you'd use is:

```
Container container = frame.getContentPane();
```

Score: _____

Notes: _____

_____

15. When you add the optional menu bar to a top-level container, is it positioned within the content pane? If not, where is it positioned?

Skill Level: Low

Expected answer: No, the optional menu bar is positioned within the top-level container, but outside of the content pane.

Score: _____

Notes: _____

_____

16. How do you create a menu separator object?

Skill Level: Low

Expected answer: A menu separator object is a normal `MenuItem` object that has a single hyphen as its string.

Score: _____

Notes: _____

_____

17. What is the immediate superclass of the Menu class?

Skill Level: Low

Expected answer: The superclass is `java.awt.MenuItem`.

Score: _____

Notes: _____

_____

18. What is the purpose of a *Layout Manager*?

Skill Level: Low

Expected answer: `Layout managers` work in conjunction with containers. A `layout manager` object performs layout management for the components within a container. All containers have a default `layout manager` associated with it, but it is easy to use another `layout manager` for a container. Layout management is the process of determining the size and location of components within a container. Other GUI applications like Borland Delphi or Visual Basic rely on exact coordinates when placing components within a container. This is not the case with Java. The `layout manager` carries out the tasks of component location and size according to guideline policies defined in the `layout manager`.

Score: _____

Notes: _____

_____

19. Name some of the Layout Managers included in Java.

Skill Level: Low

Expected answer: Some `layout managers` are:

Flow Layout Manager
Grid Layout Manager
Border Layout Manager
Box Layout Manager

Card Layout Manager
GridBag Layout Manager
Overlay Layout Manager
Spring Layout Manager (SDK 1.4+)

Score: _____

Notes: _____

_____

20. What method would you call to specify the layout manager for a container?

Skill Level: Low

Expected answer: You would call `setLayout(.)`

Score: _____

Notes: _____

_____

21. What is the default layout manager for every JPanel?

Skill Level: Low

Expected answer: The default `layout manager` is `FlowLayout`.

Score: _____

Notes: _____

_____

22. Briefly describe how the `FlowLayout` manager works.

Skill Level: Low

Expected answer: The `FlowLayout` manager will place components from left to right in a horizontal line and start new rows if necessary. The components are centered by default, but can also be aligned left or right justified.

Score: _____

Notes: _____

_____

23. What is the default Layout Manager for a JFrame's content pane?

Skill Level: Low

Expected answer: The default is `BorderLayout`.

Score: _____

Notes: _____

_____

24. What are the names of the five regions in the BorderLayout manager that are used to hold components?

Skill Level: Low

Expected answer: North, South, East, West, and Center. The constants defined for all five regions are:

BorderLayout.NORTH
BorderLayout.SOUTH
BorderLayout.EAST
BorderLayout.WEST
BorderLayout.CENTER

Score: _____

Notes: _____

_____

25. Are there any restrictions as to the number of components that can be placed in any of the regions of the BorderLayout manager? If so, what are they?

Skill Level: Low

Expected answer: First, the `BorderLayout` manager does not require that every region contain a component any of the regions can be empty.

The one strict rule is that each region can contain, at most, one component. If, for example, you attempt to add two components to the CENTER region, the last component you add will be the one that is contained in that region.

Score: _____

Notes: _____

_____

26. Of the five regions in the BorderLayout layout manager, which of the regions would be appropriate for a toolbar? A status line?

Skill Level: Low

Expected answer: The North region would be appropriate for a toolbar while the South region would be proper for a status line.

Score: _____

Notes: _____

_____

27. Is it possible to bypass the use of layout managers in and use absolute positioning of components when performing component layout? If so, then how would you go by doing this?

Skill Level: Low

Expected answer: Yes, it is possible to forgo the use of layout managers and use absolute positioning. To do this, you would first set the container's layout property to `null` and then specify the size and the position of every component within that container.

Score: _____

Notes: _____

_____

28. What is one component that every Dialog box should have?

Skill Level: Low

Expected answer: Every dialog box should contain at least an OK button used to dismiss the dialog box.

Score: _____

Notes: _____

_____

29. What is the immediate superclass of the Dialog class?

Skill Level: Low

Expected answer: `java.awt.Window`

Score: _____

Notes: _____

_____

30. What are the two methods used to hide and display a JDialog box and what package they are from?

Skill Level: Low

Expected answer: The `hide()` and `show()` methods are used to hide/display a `JDialog` box. They are both found in the `java.awt.Dialog` package.

Score: _____

Notes: _____

_____

31. What is the difference between a modal and modeless dialog box?

Skill Level: Low

Expected answer: Dialog boxes can be defined as either modal or modeless.

Modal dialog boxes, when created, block access to its parent frame. That is, the user will not be able to interact with the parent frame until the dialog box is closed.

Modeless dialog boxes do not block their parent frame in the same way, so they act more like independent windows. In practice, modal dialog boxes are easier to use and are much more common than modeless dialogs.

Score: _____

Notes: _____

_____

32. Which Swing component would you use to display hierarchical data in a tree format?

Skill Level: Low

Expected answer: `JTree`

Score: _____

Notes: _____

_____

33. Which method and value would you use for a component to disable it from receiving user input?

Skill Level: Low

Expected answer: `setEnabled(false)`

Score: _____

Notes: _____

_____

34. You want to draw a rectangle that is 10 pixels wide and 50 pixels high to the screen starting at 100 pixels down and 20 pixels over. What is the syntax to draw the rectangle?

Skill Level: Low

Expected answer:

```
g.drawRect(20, 100, 10, 50);
```

Use the `drawRect` method. The constructor for this method needs the parameters in the order `x`, `y`, `w`, `h`. The `x` value is the number of pixels over from the left to start. The Y value is the number of pixels down from the top to start. The `w` value is the width of the rectangle while `h` is the height of the rectangle.

Score: _____

Notes: _____

_____

35. What are the primary differences between Java applets and ActiveX controls?

Skill Level: Intermediate

Expected answer: Both technologies provide support for interactive Web programs similar to a GUI program developed using Java AWT/Swing. The major difference between the two is that ActiveX components rely on a system to verify the identity of ActiveX programmers plus ActiveX programs are not downloaded each time they are encountered. ActiveX also suffers from a huge security requirement in that it is not restricted in what it can do to the clients system, while Java applets face very strong and built-in restrictions on what they can do.

Score: _____

Notes: _____

_____

36. Which method of the Container class is used to cause the container to lay out its subcomponents again after the components it contains have been added to or modified?

Skill Level: Intermediate

Expected answer: The `validate()` method.

Score: _____

Notes: _____

_____

37. You have written several Listeners and added them all to the same component. Is it true that all of the Listeners will get notified of an event in the order they were added?

Skill Level: Intermediate

Expected answer: No. There is no correlation between the order that Listeners get added and the order they get notified.

Score: _____

Notes: _____

_____

38. Suppose you have an ActionListener object name buttonListener and a JButton object named button1. What statement would you use to register this button with the buttonListener?

Skill Level: Intermediate

Expected answer:

```
button1.addActionListener(buttonListener);
```

Score: _____

Notes: _____

_____

39. Briefly describe how the CardLayout layout manager works.

Skill Level: Intermediate

Expected answer: The CardLayout class is used when you need to manage two or more components (usually several JPanel containers) that need to share the same area or display space. CardLayout is useful when you have an area that contains different components that should be displayed at different times. This provides a method to manage two or more panels that need to share the same display space.

The easiest way to understand how the CardLayout layout manager works, think about traditional stack of playing cards. When the cards are stacked in a pile, only the top card is visible at any given time.

Using our playing card analogy above, here is how to choose which card (or Swing component) is visible:

You can obtain the first or last card, in the order that the cards (components) where added to the container.

You can flip through the cards (components) forward or backwards.

You can specify a card (component) with a specific name.

When you add a component to the `CardLayout` container, you need to specify a String that identifies the component.

The `CardLayout` container is usually associated with a controlling component, such as a check box or a list. The state of the controlling component determines which component the `CardLayout` displays. The user generally makes the choice by selecting something (a radio button or pull down list) within the UI.

Score: _____

Notes: _____

_____

40. What are the methods used in the CardLayout class that are used to switch from one component to another?

Skill Level: Intermediate

Expected answer:

```
void first(Container)
void last(Container)
void next(Container)
void previous(Container)
void show(Container, String)
```

Score: _____

Notes: _____

_____

41. What is the return type for all methods in all event listener interfaces in the java.awt.event package?

Skill Level: Intermediate

Expected answer: `void`

Score: _____

Notes: _____

_____

42. When implementing the ActionListener interface, what is the only method defined that has to be implemented?

Skill Level: Intermediate

Expected answer:

```
void actionPerformed(ActionEvent e)
```

The `ActionListener` interface is used for receiving action events. When the action event occurs, that object's `actionPerformed()` method is invoked.

Score: _____

Notes: _____

_____

43. Which event listener interface (listener type) would you implement with the actions to perform when a user either clicks a button, presses <RETURN> while typing in a text field, or chooses a menu item?

Conducting the Java Job Interview

Skill Level: Intermediate

Expected answer: `ActionListener`

Score: _____

Notes: _____

_____

44. Which event listener interface (listener type) would you implement with the actions to perform when a user presses a mouse button while the cursor is over a component?

Skill Level: Intermediate

Expected answer: `MouseListener`

Score: _____

Notes: _____

_____

45. Which event listener interface (listener type) would you implement with the actions to perform when a component gets keyboard focus?

Skill Level: Intermediate

Expected answer: `FocusListener`

Score: _____

Notes: _____

_____

46. Suppose you have a myMenuItem object named m on a Menu named myMenu. Write the statement that will cause the item to not appear on the Menu.

Skill Level: Intermediate

Expected answer: `remove(m);`

You can use the method remove(MenuComponent item) which is relevant to MenuItems. Remember that the methods setVisible(Boolean) and hide() only apply to Components, not MenuComponents.

Score: _____

Notes: _____

_____

47. Is it possible to determine if a user single-clicks or double-clicks a component?

Skill Level: Intermediate

Expected answer: It is possible to determine if a user single-clicked or double-clicked an object by observing the `java.awt.Event` object's `clickCount` data field.

If the user single-clicked the mouse, the `clickCount` data field will be 1 while with a double-click, `clickCount` will be 2.

Score: _____

Notes: _____

_____

48. How does the class CheckboxMenuItem relate to MenuItem?

Skill Level: Intermediate

Expected answer: The `CheckboxMenuItem` class extends `MenuItem` and supports a menu item that may be checked or unchecked.

Score: _____

Notes: _____

_____

49. What are some of the subclasses of the Component class?

Skill Level: Intermediate

Expected answer: Button, Canvas, Checkbox, Choice, Container, Label, List, Scrollbar, TextComponent

Score: _____

Notes: _____

_____

50. If you disable a lightweight component by calling setEnabled(false), can the component still receive MouseEvents?

Skill Level: High

Expected answer: Yes. The component can still receive MouseEvents if it has been disabled.

Score: _____

Notes: _____

_____

51. While a frame or dialog is running and visible, what method (not a Java method) can be used to print its component hierarchy to the standard output stream?

Skill Level: High

Expected answer: While the frame or dialog is running, click its border and then press Control-Shift F1.

Score: _____

Notes: _____

_____

52. Consider a container whose layout manager is constructed with the following statement:

```
new GridLayout(5, 10);
```

How many rows are in the container?

Skill Level: High

Expected answer: 5

Score: _____

Notes: _____

_____

53. What are the four arguments for the GridLayout manager's constructor?

Skill Level: High

Expected answer:

The four arguments for the GridLayout constructor are the number of columns and rows in the grid, and the horizontal and vertical spacing of the cells in the grid.

```
public GridLayout(int rows,
                  int cols,
                  int hgap,
                  int vgap)
```

- <u>rows</u> – number of rows, with the value zero meaning any number of rows

- <u>cols</u> – number of columns, with the value zero meaning any number of columns

- hgap - the horizontal gap
- vgap - the vertical gap

Score: _____

Notes: _____

_____

54. What does the GridBagConstraints.fill field control?

Skill Level: High

Expected answer: When a component's display area is larger than the component's requested size, the `GridBagConstraints.fill` field determines whether components will stretch vertically or horizontally to fill their cells or if they will be resized at all.

The following values are valid for the `fill` field:

- NONE: Do not resize the component.

- HORIZONTAL: Make the component wide enough to fill its display area horizontally, but do not change its height.

- VERTICAL: Make the component tall enough to fill its display area vertically, but do not change its width.

- BOTH: Make the component fill its display area entirely.

The default value is NONE.

Score: _____

Notes: _____

_____

55. How do you add components to a layout controlled by a GridBagLayout layout manager?

Skill Level: High

Expected answer: You would first initialize and set the constraints then proceed to call the `add()` method as you normally would in other layout managers.

Score: _____

Notes: _____

_____

56. What does the weightx and weighty field of the GridBagConstraints control?

Skill Level: High

Expected answer: The `weightx` field controls how a column becomes wider when its container resizes while `weighty` controls how a row becomes taller when its container resizes.

Score: _____

Notes: _____

_____

57. Assume you have an object called chooser of type JFileChooser. Is it possible to choose a directory path instead of a file path in a swing FileChooser dialog box?

Skill Level: High

Expected answer: Yes. Again, assuming you have an object instance named chooser, use the following:

```
chooser.setFileSelectionMode(
JFileChooser.DIRECTORIES_ONLY);
```

Score: _____

Notes: _____

_____

58. What interface would you implement to create a custom layout manager?

Skill Level: High

Expected answer: `LayoutManager`

Score: _____

Notes: _____

_____

59. When implementing the LayoutManager interface, what are the five methods must you provide implementations for?

Skill Level: High

Expected answer:

```
void addLayoutComponents(String, Component)
void removeLayoutComponen(Component)
Dimension preferredLayoutSize(Container)
Dimension minimumLayoutSize(Container)
void layoutContainer(Container)
```

Score: _____

Notes: _____

_____

Non-Technical Questions

When conducting an on-site or telephone interview, it's very important that you be able to assess non-technical information about your job candidate. These non-technical factors include motivation, thinking skills, and personal attitude. All of these factors have a direct bearing on the ultimate success of the candidate in your shop, and also give you an idea about the longevity of a particular client.

Each of these questions is deliberately ambiguous and probing so that the job candidate will have an opportunity to speak freely. Often these questions will give you a very good idea of the suitability of the candidate for the position. Remember, in many IT shops technical ability is secondary to the ability of the candidate to function as a team member within the organization.

1. What are your plans if you don't get this job?

   This question can reveal a great deal about the motivation of the job candidate. If the candidate indicates that he/she will change career fields, going into an unrelated position, then this person may not have a long-term motivation to stay within the IT industry. If, on the other hand, the candidate responds that he will continue to pursue opportunities within the specific technical area, then the candidate is probably dedicated to the job for which he is being interviewed.

2. How do you feel about overtime?

   This is an especially loaded question, because any honest job candidate is going to tell you that they don't like to work overtime. As we know, the reality of today's IT world is that the professional will occasionally have to work evenings and weekends. This question is essential if you're interviewing for a position that requires non-traditional hours, such as a network administrator or database administrator, where the bulk of the production changes will occur on evenings, weekends, and holidays.

3. Describe your biggest non-technical flaw.

    This question provides insight into the personality of the job candidate, as well as their honesty and candor. Responses are unpredictable and may range from "I don't suffer fools gladly" to "I have a hard time thinking after I've been on the job for 16 hours". Again, there is no right or wrong answer to this question, but it may indicate how well the candidate is going to function during critical moments. More importantly, this question gives an idea of the level of self-awareness of the candidate, and gauges whether or not they are actively working to improve their non-technical skills.

4. Describe your least favorite boss or professor.

    The answer to this question will reveal the candidate's opinions and attitudes about being supervised by others. While there is no correct response to this question, it can shed a great deal of light on the candidate's interpersonal skills.

5. Where do you plan to be ten years from now?

    This is an especially important question for the IT job candidate because it reveals a lot about their motivations. As we know, the IT job industry does not have a lot of room for advancement within the technical arena, and someone who plans to rise within the IT organization will be required to move into management at some point. It's interesting that the response to this question is often made to be overly important, especially amongst those managers that hear the response paraphrased to mean, "In ten years I would like to have your job."

6. How important is money to you?

Again, this is an extremely misleading question, because even though many IT professionals deeply enjoy their jobs, and some would even do it for free, money is a primary motivator for people in the workplace. This question provides an easy opportunity to find out whether or not your candidate is being honest with you.

An appropriate answer for the candidate might be to say that he greatly enjoys his work within IT but that he needs to be able to maintain some level of income in order to support his family. A bonus benefit of this question is it also provides insight into the demographic structure of the job candidate, namely their marital status, as well as the age of their children, and whether or not they have immediate family in the area. It's well-known within the IT industry that job candidates are most likely to remain with the company if they have a large extended family group within the immediate area.

7. Why did you leave your last job?

This is one of the most loaded questions of all, and one that can be extremely revealing about the personality of the IT job candidate. The most appropriate answer to this question is that the previous job was not technically challenging enough, or that the candidate was bored.

However, periodically you will find job candidates who will express negativity regarding the work environment, the quality of the management, and the personalities of the co-workers. This of course, should be a major red flag, because it may indicate that this job candidate does not possess the interpersonal skills required to succeed in a team environment.

8. If you were a vegetable, what vegetable would you be?

On its face, this is a totally ludicrous and ambiguous question, but it gives you an opportunity to assess the creative thinking skills of the job candidate. For example, if the job candidate merely replies "I don't know", he may not possess the necessary creative thinking skills required for a systems analyst or developer position.

A creative candidate will simply pick a vegetable, and describe in detail why that particular vegetable suits their personality. For example, the job candidate might say "I would be broccoli because I am health-oriented, have a bushy head, and go well with Chinese food".

9. Describe the month of June.

The answer to this question also provides insight into the thinking ability of the job candidate. For example, most job candidates may reply that June is a summer month, with longer days, hot weather, and an ideal vacation time. The candidate with an engineering or scientific point of view might reply instead that June is a month with 30 days, immediately preceding the summer equinox.

10. Why do you want to work here?

This is the candidate's opportunity to express why he might be a good fit for your particular organization. It also indicates whether the candidate has taken the time to research the company and the work environment. Is the candidate applying for this position solely because he needs a job, any job, or because he has specifically singled out your company due to some appealing characteristic of the work environment?

This question can also add information about the motivation of the job candidate, because a job candidate who is highly motivated to work for a particular firm will make the effort to research the company, the work environment, and even the backgrounds of individual managers.

Using a powerful search engine such as Google, the savvy IT candidate can quickly glean information about the person who is interviewing them. Having detailed knowledge of the organization is a very positive indicator that the candidate has given a lot of thought to the particular position and is evidence of high motivation.

General Questions

1. What do you know about our company?

    Answer: _____

    Comment: _____

    _____

If the prospective employee has little or no knowledge about the company, then he will also have little idea about how he can benefit the company. A candidate who has not gone to the trouble of researching the organization may be after a job, any job.

A candidate who has taken the time to explore the company will probably have specific ideas in mind about what he can bring to the organization. The initiative required by the candidate to research the company is a good sign that he is proactive and not passive dead weight.

If the candidate has some knowledge of the company's mission and function, this will also become apparent in the questions he asks you. He will already be thinking about how he can fit in and how his skills can be utilized, desirable traits of the problem-solver.

2. Why do you want to work for this company? Why should we hire you?

    Answer: _____

    Comment: _____

    _____

The answer to this question can reveal whether the candidate is merely shopping for a job or has true interest in the company and the position. It is important that the candidate show some passion for the field, if he does not, he will probably never be creative in the work environment, and he will not represent a solution for you.

Does the candidate have a core belief that his particular set of skills can benefit you? Answers such as "I believe my experience can make a difference here", or "I believe your company will provide an environment that more directly engages my interest", or "Working for your company will provide challenges that excite me" are good starters.

3. Why are you looking for a new job?

    Answer: _____

    Comment: _____

    _____

Typical reasons for seeking a new job include the desire to advance in the field and boredom in a job that offers few fresh challenges. These are positive motivations, but there can be negative ones as well. There may be personal conflicts between the candidate and other team members or management that have become so adversarial that the candidate is compelled to leave.

While not necessarily eliminating a candidate from consideration, personal friction in the previous job does raise a red flag. It may be that the candidate is an unfortunate victim of backroom politics, but if he confides in you about the shortcomings of his supervisors or fellow employees, while taking no responsibility himself, you must consider yourself warned.

4. Tell us about yourself/ your background.

    Answer: _____

    Comment: _____

    _____

This is probably asked more than any other question in interviews. It is the main opportunity for the candidate to describe his experiences, motivations, and vision of himself as it relates to the company.

The candidate should provide clear examples of how his abilities were used in the past to solve problems. If the candidate just repeats the information in the position description, he is probably only going through the motions and has no clear vision of his role in the company.

Even worse, if the candidate contradicts the job description, there is evidence of a serious problem.

5. What are the three major characteristics that you bring to the job?

Answer: _____

Comment: _____

_____

The candidate should offer specific skills or traits that he believes will be useful in the position. If the candidate is unable to relate these characteristics to the job, he has obviously not thought much about his role in the organization. You are interested in finding someone who has ideas about how he can hit the ground running and make a real difference to the company.

6. Describe the "ideal" job...the "ideal" supervisor.

Answer: _____

Comment: _____

_____

This question is not as open-ended as it may seem. If the candidate's ideal job has little or nothing in common with the position he is interviewing for, he is unlikely to be a good fit. The candidate's response should match fairly well with the requirements of the position.

The candidate's description of the ideal supervisor can provide clues about how well the candidate works with superiors. Beware the candidate who seizes this as an opportunity to denigrate past managers.

7. How would you handle a tough customer?

    Answer: _____

    Comment: _____

_____

Can the candidate provide examples of instances when difficult clients were won over? An effective communicator can strike a balance between meeting the needs of the customer and dealing with unrealistic expectations.

Above all, the candidate should indicate that he understands the necessity of "going the extra mile" to alleviate the concerns of the customer. Providing service to the client or end user is fundamental to the success of any enterprise.

8. How would you handle working with a difficult co-worker?

    Answer: _____

    Comment: _____

_____

This is similar to the last question. The candidate should relate an example of a conflict with a co-worker or team member that was successfully resolved. What you are looking for is evidence that the candidate is able to facilitate communication and lead a difficult project to a successful conclusion.

9. When would you be available to start if you were selected?

Answer: _____

Comment: _____

_____

10. How does this position match your career goals?

Answer: _____

Comment

: _____

_____

This is an excellent question to ascertain whether the candidate truly sees the position as an integral part of his career path. Does the candidate believe the knowledge and experience he will gain from this job will move him to where he wants to be?

A thorough answer to this question will lead into the next one.

11. What are your career goals (a) 3 years from now; (b) 10 years from now?

Answer: _____

Comment: _____

_____

The answer to this question will indicate the level of commitment the candidate feels towards the job and the company. If the candidate has a goal in mind, how well does it fit with the job he is applying for?

When the candidate describes his goals, does he speak in terms of the skills and abilities he hopes to acquire that will prepare him for his eventual role, or does he simply want to be the CEO, with little thought of what it might take to get there?

The interviewer may be surprised by how often the candidate will talk about goals that are unrelated to the position.

12. What do you like to do in your spare time?

Answer: _____

Comment: _____

_____

This question provides an opportunity to learn more about the character of the candidate, and to judge whether his outside interests complement his professional life. Is the candidate well-rounded or one-dimensional? Does the candidate tend to sustain an interest over time?

13. What motivates you to do a good job?

Answer: _____

Comment: _____

_____

If the candidate responds "making money" or "avoiding the wrath of my boss", you probably have a problem. The candidate should describe some positive motivation, such as a new challenge, and tie it to a specific example of a time in the past when the motivation reaped personal rewards and results on the job.

14. What two or three things are most important to you at work?

Answer: _____

Comment: _____

_____

The answer to this can reveal much about how the candidate sees himself on the job. Does the candidate mention things such as the importance of interpersonal communication, or responding quickly to crisis situations, things that facilitate job performance, or does he seem to be more worried about the timeliness of his coffee breaks?

15. What qualities do you think are essential to be successful in this kind of work?

Answer: _____

Comment: _____

_____

Does the candidate have a realistic idea of what the work environment requires of him, and do the qualities of the candidate match the job? Does the candidate have an example of a past job experience when these qualities were called upon with beneficial results?

16. How does your previous work experience prepare you for this position?

Answer: _____

Comment: _____

_____

This question relates to many of the others. If the candidate is able to articulate a clear idea of how his previous experience and training has prepared him for the responsibilities of the new position, he will be well ahead of many other interviewees.

17. How do you define "success"?

Answer: _____

Comment: _____

_____

If the answer doesn't fit the position, the candidate may be unhappy in the field, or quickly becomes bored. This indicates that the candidate may not be committed to staying with the company for very long.

18. What has been your most significant accomplishment to date?

Answer: _____

Comment: _____

_____

The candidate should be able to relate a specific example of an achievement that demonstrates a desirable quality for the job. The candidate should focus on action and results, rather than long-winded descriptions of situations.

The answer to this question can provide insight into situations that the candidate may handle especially well. The candidate should demonstrate an ability to persevere and overcome obstacles. Did the person deliver more than was expected of him in a difficult situation?

19. Describe a failure and how you dealt with it.

Answer: _____

Comment: _____

_____

This is known as a negative question, and it can be extremely revealing. It can indicate significant weaknesses or problems that may interfere with the ability to do the job.

Was the failure a catastrophic one, or a relatively minor problem? Was the candidate able to learn from the experience and apply the knowledge to future situations?

The answer to this question can also reveal how much personal accountability and responsibility the candidate accepts. If the candidate blames the failure on others, he is not likely to learn from his mistakes.

As with most interview questions, this questions is designed to provide insight into the overall personality of the candidate, and gives you a fuller appreciation of the strengths, as well as the weaknesses, of the person.

20. What leadership roles have you held?

Answer: _____

Comment: _____

_____

This answer should indicate not only that the candidate has the leadership experience to succeed in the new job, but that he has the ability to work well with others and is able to shoulder the responsibility and deal with the pressure associated with the requirements of the position.

21. Are you willing to travel?

Answer: _____

Comment: _____

_____

The answer here will demonstrate how committed to the company the candidate is likely to be. If the candidate dismisses the idea of travel completely, he may lack the motivation you are looking for.

22. What have you done in the past year to improve yourself?

Answer: _____

Comment: _____

_____

This question can shed more light on the personality of the candidate. If the candidate has been motivated by the goal of obtaining this position, he will be able to demonstrate that he has taken the initiative to prepare himself for it.

If the candidate instead chooses to describe the benefits of his basket-weaving class, he may indeed be the better for it, but it has little relevance to solving the problems he would soon encounter in the new position.

23. In what areas do you feel you need further education and training to be successful?

Answer: _____

Comment: _____

_____

If the answer has nothing to do with the offered position, the candidate may soon become bored. This question is similar to others and should dovetail with other answers about goals and career path.

24. What are your salary requirements?

Answer: _____

Comment: _____

_____

If the candidate mentions a figure that is too low, he may be uninformed or desperate. On the other hand, if his financial expectations are unreasonable, he should probably be eliminated from consideration.

The following questions are designed to zero in on key aspects of the candidate's personality and ability to perform. You may find it helpful to assign each response a score between 1 and 5 (a shorthand assessment technique that may also be used with many of the preceding questions).

Policies and Procedures

While technical expertise is essential in many IT positions, many interviews fall short in determining the discipline of a potential candidate. The questions in this section assist in determining if a potential candidate acts in accordance with established policies, procedures, and guidelines. Does he or she follow standard procedures even in crisis situations? Can they effectively communicate and enforce organizational policies and procedures along with recognizing and constructively conforming to unwritten rules?

1. Many jobs require employees to act in strict accordance with established policies. Describe to me a time when you were expected to act in accordance with policy even when it was not convenient or you disagreed with the policy. What did you do in this situation?

   Expected answer: Was the candidate able to demonstrate their commitment to follow policy even if good reasons could have been made for breaking it? Look for any non-conformity to policy because of disrespect for those who made the policy, personal style, revenge, or dishonesty?

   Score: _____

   Comment: _____

   _____

2. Many IT projects involve managing tasks and situations that involve potential for high money loss conditions. Describe a time when you have been asked to manage a situation like this and how you were able to ensure your job effectiveness.

   Expected answer: Was the candidate able to demonstrate a "no exceptions" attitude and strategy that showed systematic and rigorous use of policy, guidelines, and procedures to ensure consistency? In attempts to achieve consistency, did he or she show any "dislike" for the rules and preferences? Was there dislike for rules and preferences by the candidate for doing the job his or her own way?

Score: _____

Comment: _____

_____

3. Explain a time when you found a particular policy or procedure challenging or difficult to adhere to. How did you handle it?

Expected answer: Did the candidate take great pains to adhere to the policy and communicate the difficulty to proper management for review and/or revision? Was there an unnecessary risky deviation from policy, and no communication of either the challenge or deviation to management?

Score: _____

Comment: _____

_____

Quality

This section provides questions that help in determining the quality of potential candidates. Does he or she maintain high standards despite pressing deadlines as well as establishing high standards and measures within the organization? Look for answers that demonstrate the candidate performs work correctly the first time and inspects material for potential flaws. You also want to know that they test new methods thoroughly and reinforce excellence as a fundamental priority.

1. Explain a situation in which an important deadline was nearing, but you didn't want to compromise quality. How did you deal with it and what was its outcome?

   Expected answer: Was the candidate able to maintain high quality through investing additional resources, moving deadlines, or making a statement of work in progress? Did he or she sacrifice quality, possibly resulting in additional problems at a later time? Did the situation result in a positive outcome?

   Score: _____

   Comment: _____

   _____

2. Tell me about a situation or task you had to develop or coordinate that had to be exactly right. How did you test it and what was the outcome?

   Expected answer: Was the candidate able to rigorously identify potential sources of problems and systematically address them. Did he or she run ample trials to accurately satisfy the requirements? Look for possible problems, insufficient experimentation, or minimal piloting?

Score: _____

Comment: _____

_____

3. Describe a situation or task you were responsible for where you made quality a fundamental priority within your organization. What steps did you take to do this?

Expected answer: Was the candidate able to demonstrate systematic approaches like correction systems, control systems, error prevention systems, or even implementing training? Look for problems with their approach like haphazard or inadequate support of quality functions?

Score: _____

Comment: _____

_____

Commitment to Task

When determining a candidate's commitment to task, you need to verify their ability to take responsibility for actions and outcomes as well as their persistence despite obstacles. Will this employee be available around the clock in case of emergencies and be able to provide long hours to the job when needed. Ask questions that allow the candidate to demonstrate their dependability in difficult circumstances and if they show a sense of urgency about getting the job done.

1. Explain a difficult task or situation in which you took full responsibility for actions and outcomes. How did you act on this?

    Expected answer: Was the candidate able to publicly claim responsibility, and then cautiously manage the situation to a successful outcome. Did it involve other parties with divergent goals? Was he or she able to resolve the situation but still accepting responsibility?

    Score: _____

    Comment: _____

    _____

2. There are people that can be counted on to go the extra mile when their company really needs it. Tell me about a time when you demonstrated dependability and reliability in trying circumstances.

    Expected answer: Was the candidate able to talk about situations or task where they worked long hours to perform unique job duties to help the organization get through a personnel shortage or demanding deadlines? Did the candidate put in "extra effort" and consistently demonstrate the notion that it was not the company's problem?

Score: _____

Comment: _____

_____

3. Tell me about a time when you dedicated long hours to a job. For example, do you take work home, work on weekends or maintain long hours for system integrity or maintenance?

Expected answer: Was the candidate able to demonstrate self-direction and initiative in working particularly lengthy hours, with clear commitment to a meaningful objective? Ensure compliance to routine work requirements as well as no qualms about what was expected of them.

Score: _____

Comment: _____

_____

4. Tell me about a time when you demonstrated a sense of urgency or importance about getting results.

Expected answer: Did the candidate demonstrate that they took immediate action directed toward a specific objective, so that non-task activities and interests were given a lower priority while productivity and efficiency were given top priority? Ensure they were able to clearly explain their emphasis on effectiveness, speed, and efficiency.

Score: _____

Comment: _____

_____

Planning, Prioritizing and Goal Setting

Questions in this category demonstrate a candidate's ability to prepare for emerging customer needs, manage multiple projects, and determine project urgency in a meaningful and sensible way. Look for their use of goals to guide actions and create detailed action plans, organize and schedule tasks and people.

1. Tell me about a situation that explains how well you manage multiple projects at one time.

   Expected answer: Was the candidate able to keep all projects moving at a pace to hit deadlines and in a systematic, manageable, quality way using a meaningful approach to prioritizing? Was there haphazard allotment of resources to different tasks, with unproductive and unnecessary chaos?

   Score: _____

   Comment: _____

   _____

2. Many factors can help in setting meaningful priorities based on ease of task, customer size, deadlines, etc. Tell me about a time when it was challenging for you to prioritize.

   Expected answer: Did the candidate use a sensible set of priorities and apply them consistently? Make sure that the candidate does not demonstrate excess bouncing of resources, resulting in inefficiencies, or a poor choice of criteria on which to prioritize.

   Score: _____

   Comment: _____

   _____

3. Describe a project in which you proficiently coordinated tasks, people, and schedules. How did you perform in this situation and what was the outcome?

   Expected answer: Did the candidate use a systematic and concentrated approach to identify tasks, people who can perform the tasks, adjusting schedules, and project constraints? Ensure that their steps were not an overly simplistic approach that was inadequate given the complexities of the project.

   Score: _____

   Comment: _____

   _____

Attention to Detail

The questions in this section help to determine the candidate's ability to be "alert" in high-risk environments. Does he or she consistently follow detailed procedures and ensure accuracy in documentation and data. Do they carefully monitor reports, processes, system performance and concentrate on routine work details plus organize and maintain a system of records.

1. Explain a time when you were tasked to apply changes to a mission critical and potentially high money loss system. What steps did you take to insure the stability and integrity of the system? What procedures did you take to ensure a successful outcome and what were the results?

    Expected answer: Ensure the candidate dutifully monitored all potentially troublesome aspects of the environment, and addressed anything that was not perfect. Did the candidate take careful steps and remain aware of potential trouble spots, and not rely on subsequent quick reactions in favor of prevention?

    Score: _____

    Comment: _____

    _____

2. Tell me about an experience from your past, which illustrates your ability to be attentive to details when monitoring a mission critical system. Explain the details of how you approached this and what were the results.

    Expected answer: Was the candidate able to demonstrate commitment to monitoring and understanding the system and to using a well thought out strategy to ensure/enhance attention to detail? Also question that the candidate was not "overconfident" and giving little awareness of potential distractions.

Score: _____

Comment: _____

_____

3. How do you go about ensuring accuracy and consistency in situations or tasks as in preparing a document or ensuring system integrity? Describe a specific case in which your attention to detail paid off.

Expected answer: Was the candidate able to take clear and consistent precautions such as proofing thoroughly, double-checking, verifying format consistency, etc.? Was there only a cursory spot check or did they check and double-check accuracy?

Score: _____

Comment: _____

_____

4. Do you have problems in dealing with "routine work"? Describe your experiences in coping with routine work. What kinds of problems did you have to overcome in order to focus and concentrate on the details of the job?

Expected answer: Was the candidate able to use strategic means to maintain attentiveness and focus during routine work? Did he or she show any diminished alertness, with little effort being made to remove or reduce it?

Score: _____

Comment: _____

_____

5. Tell me about a situation or task that demonstrates your ability to organize and maintain a system of records.

   Expected answer: Was the candidate able to initiate or illustrate commitment to a systematic method for organization and record keeping? Look for possible ineffectiveness record keeping, or overconfidence on human memory, or dependence on others?

   Score: _____

   Comment: _____

   _____

Self-Initiative

Self-initiative is a valuable asset in any employee. Questions in this category should test potential candidates by asking them about times when they undertook additional responsibilities and were able to respond to situations as they arose with no supervision. Does this candidate demonstrate the ability to bring about significant results from ordinary circumstances? Do they prepare for problems or opportunities in advance?

1. Describe to me a situation in which you assertively capitalized on an opportunity and converted something ordinary into something extraordinary?

   Expected answer: Was the candidate able to demonstrate a time when they took an ordinary and routine situation and were able to put forth a unique solution that yielded positive results. It should be a unique solution that may not have been achieved by others given the same situation? Was the outcome of the accomplishment of little magnitude or what would have been expected of anyone in that situation?

   Score: _____

   Comment: _____

   _____

2. Describe a situation where you responded to a situation as it arose with little or no supervision.

   Expected answer: Was the candidate able to demonstrate a situation where they took reasonable, quick and decisive action given an appropriate amount of information or research, affirming their independence? Pay attention to their use of authority – was it appropriate? Did the candidate make good decisions with little procrastination?

Score: _____

Comment: _____

_____

3. Tell me about a time when you voluntarily took on a special project that was above and beyond your normal responsibilities.

Expected answer: Despite an already full workload, did the candidate still volunteer for a large or complex task? Where they able to successfully complete the task without undue compromise of other responsibilities? Verify the candidate did not unnecessarily sacrifice other areas of responsibilities.

Score: _____

Comment: _____

_____

4. Many people contend to have good ideas, but so few act on them. Describe to me how you've transformed a good idea into a productive and beneficial business outcome.

Expected answer: Did the candidate produce an organized and meaningful action plan to bring their idea to fruition? Verify that the action plan was organized, realistic and productive.

Score: _____

Comment: _____

_____

Conducting the Java Job Interview

Index

About Jeffrey Hunter

Jeffrey Hunter graduated from Stanislaus State University in Turlock California with a Bachelor's degree in Computer Science. Jeff is an Oracle Certified Professional, Java Development Certified Professional, and currently works as an independent Senior Database Administrator.

His work includes advanced performance tuning, Java programming, capacity planning, database security, and physical / logical database design in a UNIX, Linux, and Windows NT environment. Jeff's other interests include mathematical encryption theory, programming language processors (compilers and interpreters) in Java and C, LDAP, writing web-based database administration tools, Xemacs and of course Linux.

About Mike Reed

When he first started drawing, Mike Reed drew just to amuse himself. It wasn't long, though, before he knew he wanted to be an artist.

Today he does illustrations for children's books, magazines, catalogs, and ads.

He also teaches illustration at the College of Visual Art in St. Paul, Minnesota. Mike Reed says, "Making pictures is like acting — you can paint yourself into the action." He often paints on the computer, but he also draws in pen and ink and paints in acrylics. He feels that learning to draw well is the key to being a successful artist.

Mike is regarded as one of the nation's premier illustrators and is the creator of the popular "Flame Warriors" illustrations at **www.flamewarriors.com**. A renowned children's artist, Mike has also provided the illustrations for dozens of children's books.

Mike Reed has always enjoyed reading. As a young child, he liked the Dr. Seuss books. Later, he started reading biographies and war stories. One reason why he feels lucky to be an illustrator is because he can listen to books on tape while he works. Mike is available to provide custom illustrations for all manner of publications at reasonable prices. Mike can be reached at **www.mikereedillustration.com**.

Conducting the Oracle Job Interview

IT Manager's Guide for Oracle Job Interviews with Oracle Interview Questions

Mike Ault & Don Burleson

ISBN 0-9727513-1-9
Publication Date – February, 2003

Retail Price $16.95 / £10.95

As professional consultants, Don Burleson and Mike Ault have interviewed hundreds of Oracle job candidates. With over four decades of interviewing experience, Ault and Burleson tell you how to quickly identify acceptable Oracle job candidates by asking the right Oracle job interview questions.

Mike Ault and Don Burleson are recognized as the two best-selling Oracle Authors in the world. With combined authorship of over 25 books, Ault & Burleson are the two most respected Oracle authorities on the planet. For the first time ever, Ault & Burleson combine their talents in this exceptional handbook.

Using Oracle job interview questions that are not available to the general public, the IT manager will be able to quickly access the technical ability of any Oracle job candidate. In today's market, there are thousands of under-trained Oracle professionals, and the IT manager must be able to quickly access the true ability of the Oracle job candidate.

www.Rampant-Books.com

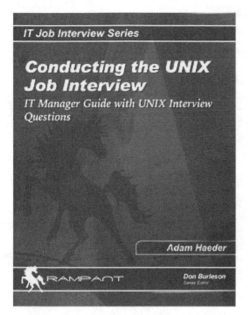

Conducting the UNIX Job Interview

IT Manager Guide with UNIX Interview Questions

Adam Haeder

ISBN 0-9744355-6-2

Retail Price $16.95 / £10.95

This book is the accumulated observations of the authors' interviews with hundreds of job candidates. The author provides useful insights into what characteristics make a good UNIX programmer and offer their accumulated techniques as an aid to interviewing an UNIX job candidate.

This handy guide has a complete set of UNIX job interview questions and provides a complete method for accurately accessing the technical abilities of UNIX job candidates. By using UNIX job interview questions that only an experienced person knows, your supervisor can ask the right interview questions and fill your UNIX job with the best qualified UNIX developer.

- Assists the IT manager in choosing the best-qualified UNIX professionals.

- Provides proven techniques that can accurately ascertain a job candidate's suitability for an UNIX position.

www.Rampant-Books.com

Conducting the Computer Programmer Job Interview

IT Manager Guide with C, C++, Cobol, UNIX shell & Oracle Interview Questions

April Wells

ISBN 0-9745993-2-8

Retail Price $16.95 / £10.95

This book is the accumulated observations of the authors' programmer job interviews with hundreds of job candidates. The author provides useful insights into what characteristics make a good computer programmer, and offer their accumulated techniques as an aid to interviewing a programmer job candidate.

This handy guide has a complete set of programmer job interview questions and provides a complete method for accurately accessing the technical abilities of programmer job candidates. By using computer programmer job interview questions that only an experienced programmer knows, you can ask the right interview questions and fill your programmer job with the best qualified programmer.

www.Rampant-Books.com

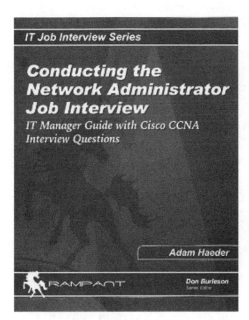

Conducting the Network Administrator Job Interview

IT Manager Guide with Cisco CCNA Interview Questions

Adam Haeder

ISBN 0-9744355-7-0

Retail Price $16.95 / £10.95

This book is the accumulated observations of the authors' interviews with hundreds of job candidates. The author provides useful insights into what characteristics make a good Network Administrator programmer and offer their accumulated techniques as an aid to interviewing an Network Administrator job candidate.

This handy guide has a complete set of Network Administrator job interview questions and provides a complete method for accurately accessing the technical abilities of Network Administrator job candidates. By using Network Administrator job interview questions that only an experienced person knows, your supervisor can ask the right interview questions and fill your Network Administrator job with the best qualified Network Administrator developer.

www.Rampant-Books.com

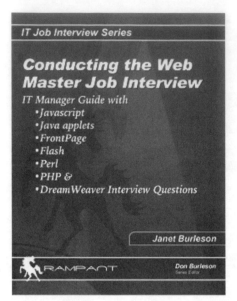

Conducting the Web Master Job Interview

IT Manager Guide with Interview Questions

Janet Burleson

ISBN 0-9745993-1-X

Retail Price $16.95 / £10.95

As a professional web master, Janet Burleson has extensive experience interviewing web master job candidates. With over a decade of interviewing experience, Burleson tell you how to quickly identify acceptable web master job candidates by asking the right web master job interview questions.

This book is the accumulated observations of the author's interviews with hundreds of job candidates. The author provides useful insights into what characteristics make a good web master programmer and offers her accumulated techniques as an aid to interviewing a web master job candidate.

This handy guide has a complete set of web master job interview questions and provides a complete method for accurately assessing the technical abilities of web master job candidates. By using web master job interview questions that only an experienced person knows, your supervisor can ask the right interview questions and fill your web master job with the best qualified web master developer.

www.Rampant-Books.com

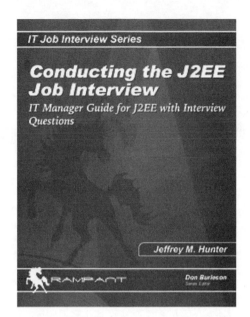

Conducting the J2EE Job Interview

IT Manager Guide for J2EE with Interview Questions

Jeffrey M. Hunter

ISBN 0-9744355-9-7

Retail Price $27.95

This book is the accumulated observations of the author's interviews with hundreds of job candidates. The author provides useful insights into what characteristics make a good J2EE programmer and offers his accumulated techniques as an aid to interviewing a J2EE programmer job candidate.

This handy guide has a complete set of J2EE job interview questions and provides a complete method for accurately assessing the technical abilities of J2EE job candidates. By using J2EE job interview questions that only an experienced person knows, your application developers can ask the right interview questions and fill your J2EE job with the best qualified J233 developer.

www.Rampant-Books.com

The Oracle In-Focus Series

The *Oracle In-Focus* series is a unique publishing paradigm, targeted at Oracle professionals who need fast and accurate working examples of complex issues. *Oracle In-Focus* books are unique because they have a super-tight focus and quickly provide Oracle professionals with what they need to solve their problems.

Oracle In-Focus books are designed for the practicing Oracle professional. Oracle In-Focus books are an affordable way for all Oracle professionals to get the information they need, and get it fast.

Expert Authors – All *Oracle In-Focus* authors are content experts and are carefully screened for technical ability and communications skills.

Online Code Depot – All code scripts from *Oracle In-Focus* are available on the web for instant download. Those who purchase a book will get the URL and password to download their scripts.

Lots of working examples – *Oracle In-Focus* is packed with working examples and pragmatic tips.

No theory – Practicing Oracle professionals know the concepts, they need working code to get started fast.

Concise – Most *Oracle In-Focus* books are less than 200 pages and get right to-the-point of the tough technical issues.

Tight focus - The *Oracle In-Focus* series addresses tight topics and targets specific technical areas of Oracle technology.

Affordable – Reasonably priced, *Oracle In-Focus* books are the perfect solution to challenging technical issues.

http://www.Rampant-Books.com